CIRCULAR WALKS ALONG THE CHILTERN WAY

Hertfordshire & Bedfordshire

Nick Moon

The Chiltern Way was established by the Chiltern Society to mark the Millennium by providing walkers in the twenty-first century with a new way of exploring the diverse, beautiful countryside which the Chilterns have to offer. Based on the idea of the late Jimmy Parsons' Chiltern Hundred but expanded at the suggestion of Rob Bethell to cover the whole Chilterns, the route was largely devised by the author, while Rob Bethell masterminded the signposting, waymarking and improvement of the route on the Society's Rights of Way Group's behalf in preparation for the Way's formal launch in October 2000. In 2003, following the success of the original route, further loops were added extending the Way to both extremities of the Chilterns including the beautiful Oxfordshire section of the Thames Valley and the spectacular downland of the Barton Hills and in 2010, to mark its tenth anniversary, a further alternative loop has been created to take in the scenic Berkshire hills between Cookham and Henley.

As many walkers want to explore the Way in half- or full-day sections without having to walk back by the same route or rely on public transport which may, in rural areas, be infrequent or non-existent, especially on Sundays, it was decided to produce two volumes, each containing 20 circular walks incorporating sections of the original Way or its Extensions, to meet this need and now a third is in preparation to include the Berkshire Loop. While they cannot take in anything like the total 220-mile length of the Way and its variants, they include some of its best sections and give the walker a representative impression of the route as a whole.

The author, Nick Moon, has lived in or regularly visited the Chilterns all his life and has, for many years, been an active member of the Chiltern Society's Rights of Way Group, which seeks to protect and improve the area's path and bridleway network. Thanks to the help and encouragement of the late Don Gresswell MBE, he was introduced to the writing of books of walks and has since written or contributed to a number of publications in this field.

1

OTHER PUBLICATIONS BY NICK MOON

The Chiltern Way including the Extensions & Berkshire Loop
The Chiltern Society (new edition due) 2014

Circular Walks along the Chiltern Way
Volume 1:   Buckinghamshire and Oxfordshire:
                     Book Castle (new edition) 2010
Volume 2:   Hertfordshire and Bedfordshire:
                     The Chiltern Society (new edition) 2014

Chiltern Walks Trilogy
Chiltern Walks 1:   Hertfordshire, Bedfordshire and
                     North Buckinghamshire:
                     Book Castle (new edition) 2007
Chiltern Walks 2:   Buckinghamshire:
                     Book Castle (new edition) 2010
Chiltern Walks 3:   Oxfordshire and West Buckinghamshire:
                     The Chiltern Society (new edition) 2001

Family Walks
Family Walks 1:   Chilterns - South : Book Castle 1997
Family Walks 2:   Chilterns - North : Book Castle 1998

Oxfordshire Walks
Oxfordshire Walks 1: Oxford, The Cotswolds and The Cherwell
                     Valley: Book Castle (new edition) 1998
Oxfordshire Walks 2: Oxford, The Downs and The Thames Valley:
                     Book Castle (new edition) 2002

The d'Arcy Dalton Way across the Oxfordshire Cotswolds and
    Thames Valley : CPRE Oxfordshire (new edition due) 2014

First published April 2005   New edition October 2014

by The Chiltern Society, White Hill Centre, White Hill, Chesham,
Bucks HP5 1AG. www.chilternsociety.org.uk

© Nick Moon

ISBN 978 0 904148 15 2

Contents

CIRCULAR WALKS ALONG THE CHILTERN WAY 2 : HERTFORDSHIRE & BEDFORDSHIRE

LIST OF WALKS

3

POSSIBLE LONGER WALKS PRODUCED BY COMBINING WALKS DESCRIBED IN THE BOOK

Walks			Miles	Km
3	+ 16		13.3	21.4
3	+ 16	+ 15	19.5	31.4
6	+ 7		14.6	23.5
11	+ 12A		15.7	25.2
11	+ 12A	+ 13	21.9	35.3
11	+ 12B		13.1	21.1
12A	+ 13		14.7	23.7
12 (A-B)	+ 13		10.1	16.3
19	+ 20		11.7	18.8

Cover photograph : Leaving Chipperfield (Walk 18)

© Nick Moon

4

Introduction

The Chiltern Way, which was created by the Chiltern Society as its Millennium project, is based on the idea of the late Jimmy Parsons' 'Chiltern Hundred`, but, whereas Jimmy's route was confined to a 100-mile circuit of the central Chilterns, the original Chiltern Way takes in four Chiltern counties in a 133-mile circuit extending from Ewelme, Oxfordshire in the southwest to Sharpenhoe Clappers, Bedfordshire and Lilley, Hertfordshire in the northeast as well as going as far southeast as Chorleywood West on the Chiltern downslope. The extensions lengthen the route to 172 miles and take it southwards to the Thames at Mapledurham and Goring and eastwards via the Barton Hills almost to Hitchin, while a route via the Berkshire Loop and extensions is of similar length and takes in the scenic hills between Cookham and Henley.

The walks in this book range in length from 5.4 to 9.2 miles and thus form a comfortable half-day walk to a leisurely full-day walk. In addition, details of several possible combinations of walks of up to 22 miles are provided for those wishing a longer, more challenging walk.

Details of how to reach the starting points by car and where to park are given in the introductory information to each walk and any convenient railway stations are shown on the accompanying plan. For up-to-date information on bus services consult the Traveline website at <www.traveline.org.uk> or call their telephone hotline on 0871-200 22 33.

All the walks described here follow public rights of way, use recognised permissive paths or cross public open space. As the majority of walks cross land used for economic purposes such as agriculture, forestry or the rearing of game, walkers are urged to follow the Country Code at all times:-

- Be **safe** - plan ahead and follow any signs.
- **Leave** gates and property as you find them.
- **Protect** plants and animals, and take your litter home.
- Keep dogs under close **control**.
- **Consider** other people.

Observing these rules helps prevent financial loss to landowners and damage to the environment, as well as the all-too-frequent and sometimes justified bad feeling towards walkers in the countryside.

While it is hoped that the special maps provided with each walk will assist the user to complete the walks without going astray and skeleton details of the surrounding road network are given to enable walkers to shorten the routes in emergency, it is always advisable to take an

Ordnance Survey or Chiltern Society map with you to enable you to shorten or otherwise vary the routes without using roads or get your bearings if you do become seriously lost. Details of the appropriate maps are given in the introductory information of each walk.

As for other equipment, readers are advised that some mud will normally be encountered on most walks particularly in woodland except in the driest weather. However proper walking boots are to be recommended at all times as, even when there are no mud problems, hard ruts or rough surfaces make the protection given by boots to the ankles desirable. In addition, the nature of the countryside makes many Chiltern paths prone to overgrowth, particularly in summer. To avoid resultant discomfort, protective clothing is advisable, especially where specific warnings are given.

In order to assist in coordinating the plans and the texts, all the numbers of path used have been shown on the plans and incorporated into the texts. These numbers, which are also shown on the Chiltern Society's series of footpath maps, consist of the official County Council footpath number with prefix letters used to indicate the parish concerned. It is therefore most helpful to use these when reporting any path problems you may find, together, if possible, with the national grid reference for the precise location of the trouble spot, as, in this way, the problem can be identified on the ground with a minimum of time loss in looking for it. National grid references can only be calculated with the help of Ordnance Survey Landranger or Explorer maps and some recent editions of Chiltern Society maps and an explanation of how this is done can be found in the Key to all current Ordnance Survey maps.

The length of time required for any particular walk depends on a number of factors such as your personal walking speed, the number of hills, stiles, etc. to be negotiated, whether or not you stop to rest, eat or drink, investigate places of interest, etc. and the number of impediments such as mud, crops, overgrowth, ploughing, etc. which you encounter, but generally an average speed of between two and two and a half miles per hour is about right in the Chilterns. It is, however, always advisable to allow extra time if you are limited by the daylight or catching a particular bus or train home in order to avoid your walk developing into a race against the clock.

Should you have problems with any of the paths used on the walks or find that the description given is no longer correct, the author would be most grateful if you could let him have details (c/o Chiltern Society), so that attempts can be made to rectify the problem or the text can be corrected at the next reprint. Nevertheless, the author hopes that you will not encounter any serious problems and have pleasure from following the walks.

Chiltern
Society

The Chiltern Society aims to conserve and protect the natural beauty, environment and heritage of the Chilterns. The Society's Rights of Way Group actively protects and restores open access land and public rights of way in the Chilterns — some 5,000 paths. It has surveyed every individual path and takes up irregularities with parish, district or county councils to preserve and enhance public rights. The charity has over 6,500 members and organises weekly walks and cycle rides, as well as volunteer work parties to carry out footpath maintenance and other conservation projects.

We welcome new members - come and join people like you who love the Chilterns. For more details please contact:

Chiltern Society,
The White Hill Centre,
White Hill,
Chesham,
Buckinghamshire HP5 1AG.

Tel. : 01494-771250.
Email : office@chilternsociety.org.uk
Website : www.chilternsociety.org.uk

INDEX MAP

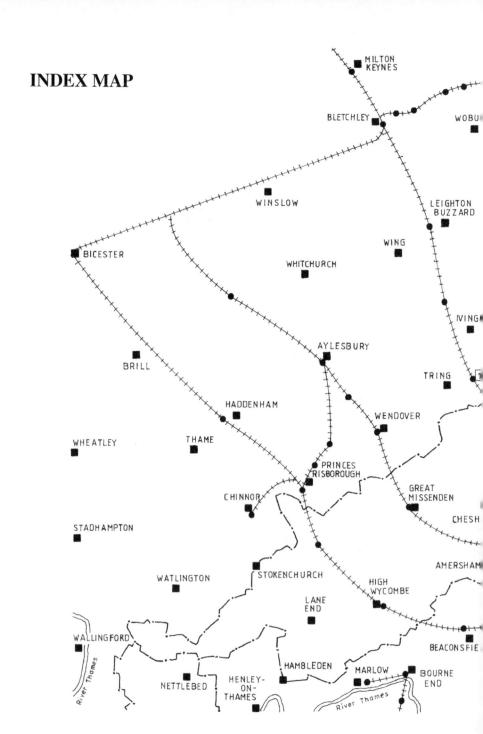

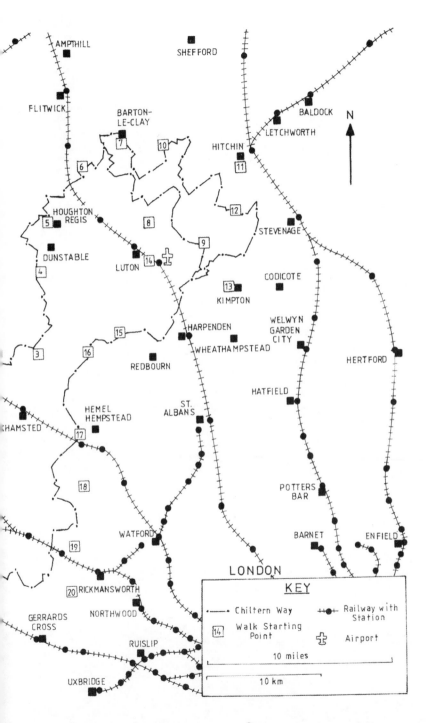

AMPTHILL

SHEFFORD

FLITWICK

BARTON-
LE-CLAY

[7]

[10]

HITCHIN

[11]

BALDOCK

LETCHWORTH

N

[6]

[12]

HOUGHTON
REGIS

[5]

[8]

[9]

STEVENAGE

DUNSTABLE

LUTON

[14]

CODICOTE

[4]

[13]

KIMPTON

WELWYN
GARDEN
CITY

[15]

HARPENDEN

[16]

WHEATHAMPSTEAD

[3]

REDBOURN

HERTFORD

HATFIELD

HEMEL
HEMPSTEAD

ST.
ALBANS

KHAMSTED

[17]

[18]

POTTERS
BAR

WATFORD

BARNET

ENFIELD

[19]

LONDON

[20] RICKMANSWORTH

KEY

NORTHWOOD

•—— Chiltern Way ++•+ Railway with
Station

GERRARDS
CROSS

[14] Walk Starting
Point

✠ Airport

RUISLIP

10 miles

UXBRIDGE

10 km

WALK 1	Tring Station

Length of Walk: 7.1 miles / 11.4 Km
Starting Point: Entrance to Tring Station.
Grid Ref: SP951123
Maps: OS Landranger Sheet 165
OS Explorer Sheet 181
Chiltern Society FP Maps Nos. 18 & 19
How to get there / Parking: Tring Station, 1.7 miles northeast
of the centre of Tring, may be reached from the town by
taking the road signposted to Tring Station and Aldbury to
Tring Station where you pass the station and cross the
railway bridge and the station car park is on your right.
On-street parking near the station is also possible except on
weekday mornings.

Tring Station, on the L&NWR Euston-Birmingham main line, built
in 1838 and now known as the West Coast main line, was, like
many Victorian railway stations, some distance from the settlement
it served and indeed was so far from the town as to be in the
neighbouring parish of Aldbury. The town itself, situated at a gap
in the Chiltern escarpment, has, indeed, always been a place of
some importance, as it straddles Akeman Street, a Roman road
from London to Cirencester near its junction with the Ancient
British Upper Icknield Way, which also passes through the suburbs
of the town. In more modern times, Tring, as well as being on the
West Coast main line, has found itself on the routes of various
generations of main traffic arteries in the form of the A41 trunk
road from London to Aylesbury and Birmingham and the Grand
Union Canal from London to the Midlands. The town boasts a
principally fifteenth-century church with a Grinling Gibbons
monument from 1707 to Sir William Gore, the first Director of the
Bank of England. Not far from the town centre is a large mansion
called Tring Park, originally built for Sir William Gore by Sir
Christopher Wren. This house, reputedly often visited in its early
years by Nell Gwynne, was the home of the Gore family for two
centuries, before being acquired in 1873 by the Rothschilds, who
enlarged it giving it its Victorian appearance. The surrounding
park, through the upper part of which the walk passes, was largely
severed from the house in the 1970s by the building of the Tring

Bypass, but, while this road ruined its open lower part, it did not affect the wooded upland area near Wigginton.

The walk, which is one of considerable variety, first leads you from Tring Station along the Ridgeway through the former park of Pendley Manor before climbing with fine views to the hilltop village of Wigginton. You then continue through woodland in Tring Park to Hastoe, the highest village in Hertfordshire. Leaving the Ridgeway, the walk now turns south to join the Chiltern Way and follow it eastwards along Grim's Ditch to skirt Wigginton, before descending through woodland to Cow Roast. Here you leave the Chiltern Way and take the Grand Union Canal towpath back to your starting point.

Starting from the entrance to Tring Station, turn left into Station Road, joining the Ridgeway. Having crossed a bridge over the Grand Union Canal, turn left into Beggars Lane. After 200 yards, turn right through gates onto path AB66, ignoring a crossing riding track and taking a fenced path straight on with views of Pendley Farm and later Pendley Manor to your right. On reaching a macadam drive to your right, take a fenced gravel track straight on with views over your left shoulder towards Aldbury and the Bridgewater Monument in trees to the left of it. Where the track bears left, go straight on through a kissing-gate and follow a fenced path along the edge of a tree belt to reach gates onto the A4251 (formerly the A41) on the course of ancient Akeman Street.

Cross this road by way of a nearby traffic island and turn right along a short section of roadside footway. Where the footway ends, turn left onto path WG14, climbing steeply and passing left of a gate to reach a kissing-gate left of padlocked gates. Now take a fenced path uphill to another kissing-gate, where you bear right to reach a spectacular high footbridge over the A41 giving fine views to your left down the Bulbourne valley towards Northchurch and Berkhamsted, to your right towards Tring and behind you towards Pitstone Hill, Clipper Down, the Bridgewater Monument and Aldbury. At the far end of the bridge, go through a kissing-gate, then take a fenced path, bearing right then left to another kissing-gate. Here take a fenced path straight on to a further kissing-gate between lightning-damaged trees, then continue with fine views to your left towards Northchurch and Berkhamsted to gates onto a road called The Twist. Turn right onto this road, then immediately left up steps and through a kissing-gate onto path WG20, soon following a right-hand fence with fine views across Tring to your right. Now follow the edge of Langton Wood, then a right-hand hedge to another kissing-gate, then bear right, following a right-hand hedge past two fields skirting a copse. On going through a further kissing-gate, more fine views open out to your right across Tring, soon with Pitstone Hill and Clipper Down coming into view farther to the right. Now continue beside a left-hand fence then a hedge, passing an old triangulation post and eventually reaching a kissing-gate into Fox Lane on the edge of Wigginton.

Wigginton, a hilltop village above Tring with superb views across the surrounding countryside, was, at one time, very much an estate village housing workers from Lord Rothschild's estate at Tring Park and many of its sturdy nineteenth-century cottages were, indeed, originally built by this benevolent estate. Just to the south is the well-known health farm of Champneys in a house also dating from this period, while the mediæval parish church was largely rebuilt in 1881, but retains the fifteenth-century West Chamber. Like many other villages in the northern Chilterns, Wigginton was, in the nineteenth century, also a centre for straw-plaiting which supplied the hat-making industry of Luton and Dunstable.

Cross this road and take path WG18 straight on up a gravel track past some cottages to a gate and gaps into woodland in Tring Park. Here ignore a branching path to your left and take path TU21 straight on along a flinty track. After 100 yards, at a five-way junction, turn left onto path TU85, following a flinty track within an avenue of tall limes obscured by other encroaching trees and bushes for about two-thirds of a mile, eventually passing a seat where there is a fine view across Tring with Tring Park House in the foreground and Mentmore Towers in the trees beyond, another Rothschild mansion, built between 1851 and 1854 for Baron Mayer de Rothschild by Sir Joseph Paxton, designer of the Crystal Palace, and his son, George Stokes. Where the avenue ends, continue to follow the stone track, ignoring branching paths to right and left, then bearing left and eventually reaching a gate and gaps leading to a road called Marlin Hill, onto which you turn left.

At a road junction on the edge of Hastoe, at 770 feet the highest village in Hertfordshire, leaving the Ridgeway, keep straight on, passing Wick Wood to your left and reaching a corner of a wood called High Scrubs to your right. Here, **joining the Chiltern Way**, turn left over a stile onto path TU13, following Grim's Ditch through Wick Wood, then generally along the edge of a tree belt. Grim's Ditch is an ancient earthwork of unknown origin which is, however, believed to date from before the Saxon period as ´Grim` is an alternative name for the Germanic god, Wodan, and they are unlikely to have attributed something to a god which they had built themselves. Where the trees peter out, take a grassy track straight on until you reach a hedge, then turn right and follow it for 35 yards. Now turn left through a kissing-gate onto path WG17 and go straight across a field to a kissing-gate onto Chesham Road on the edge of Wigginton, where the ´Greyhound` is a third of a mile to your left.

Turn right into Chesham Road. After 20 yards, turn left through a kissing-gate onto path WG21 through a copse, then between a hedge and a fence, eventually reaching a road at Wigginton Bottom. Turn left onto this road, then, in the bottom of a dip, turn right onto path WG5 along a short lane into a field. Here take the right-hand grassy track uphill beside a right-hand hedge then a fence, then keep straight on to rejoin the hedge by some ash trees. Now follow it, bearing right into a green lane, along which you continue until you reach a stile by gates into Lower Wood. Here keep right at a fork and take path WG6 generally straight on through the wood, eventually descending into a valley bottom. At a T-junction, turn right onto path WG8, soon leaving the wood by a kissing-gate and following a left-hand fence straight on to a gate and kissing-gate at the far end of the field. Now go straight on across the next field to a kissing-gate into a green lane (path WG11). Turn right into this lane, soon becoming a concrete road and bearing right beside the A41 Berkhamsted Bypass, then dropping to reach Bottom House Lane.

Turn left onto this road, passing under the A41 bridge, then, by a large house called Tinker's Lodge, turn right onto byway WG10, following its drive at first, then continuing along a rough lane. After this bears left, ignore a branching path to your right and keep straight on for a third of a mile, eventually reaching the A4251 at Cow Roast by the ´Cow Roast Inn`. The inn, after which the hamlet is named, is thought originally to have been called the ´Cow Rest` and to have been a resting place for cattle drovers on their way along the main road to London.

Here turn right onto the A4251, then, just past the inn, turn left onto a narrow road crossing a bridge over the Grand Union Canal by Cow Roast Lock. Originally named the Grand Junction Canal, the Grand Union Canal was built by the third Duke of Bridgewater and his engineer friend, James Brindley, between 1793 and 1806 in order to improve freight transport between London and the industrial Midlands and North in the days before the railways had been conceived of and it only received its present name in 1929. Here, **leaving the Chiltern Way**, turn left down a ramp between walls to reach the lock, then take the canal towpath straight on for 1.4 miles to the second crossing road bridge. Having passed under this bridge, turn sharp right up a flight of steps to reach Station Road, then turn left for Tring Station.

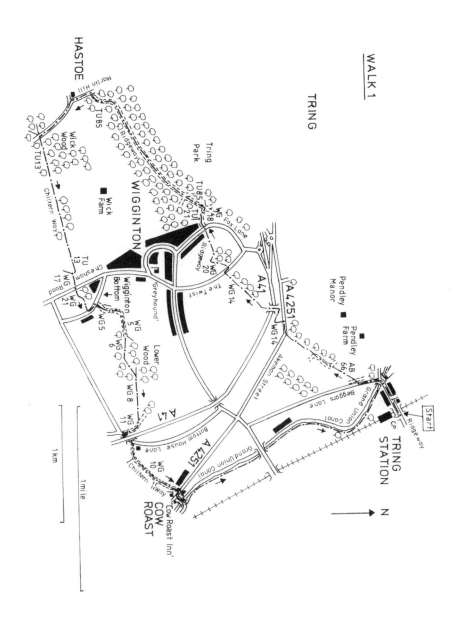

WALK 1

TRING

HASTOE

Martin Hill

TU85

Wick Wood

TU13

Chiltern Way

Tring Park

WIGGINTON

Wick Farm

TU85 TU1
WG21

TU 13

Chesham Rd

WG 17

WG 21

WG5

Ridgeway

Greyhound'

Wigginton Bottom

WG 5

WG 6

WG 8

WG 11

Lower Wood

A.41

WG 18 Fox Lane

WG 20

Ridgeway

The Twist

WG 14

A41

A 4251

WG14

Akeman Street

Pendley Manor

Pendley Farm

AB 66

Beggars Lane

Grand Union Canal

Start

Ridgeway

TRING STATION

CP

Bottom House Lane

A 4251

WG 10

Chiltern Way

Cow Roast Inn'

COW ROAST

Grand Union Canal

N

1 km

1 mile

15

WALK 2   Aldbury Common

Length of Walk: 5.3 miles / 8.5 Km
Starting Point: End of the road to the Bridgewater Monument on Aldbury Common.
Grid Ref: SP971131
Maps: OS Landranger Sheet 165
OS Explorer Sheet 181
Chiltern Society FP Map No.19
How to get there / Parking: The Bridgewater Monument, 3.5 miles northwest of Berkhamsted, may be reached from the town by taking the A4251 to Northchurch, then turning right onto the B4506 and following it for 2.7 miles. Some two-thirds of a mile past the Aldbury turn, turn left onto the macadam road to the Bridgewater Monument and park as close as you can to its far end.

Aldbury Common is one of a belt of several mostly wooded commons extending from the outskirts of Berkhamsted to Aldbury village and across the Bucks boundary to the Chiltern escarpment. When the Ashridge Estate was sold in 1929, a large area of these commons was acquired by the National Trust which has done much to facilitate public access. Ashridge House, which can be seen at the other end of Prince's Riding (from where the car park is located) and has been variously described as being ´like a snowman, built up by sticking on lumps instead of having good bones inside it` and by the Chiltern writer, H.J. Massingham as being ´like a gigantic wedding cake` and ´hideous but ... also comic`, was commissioned by the third Duke of Bridgewater before his death in 1803 to replace a mediæval house, which had passed to his family in 1604 and had formerly been a monastery. Designed in the neo-Gothic style by James Wyatt and his nephew, Sir Jeffry Wyatville, it was eventually completed in about 1820. The Bridgewater Monument, at the opposite end of the Riding where the walk starts, is a tall Doric column also designed by Sir Jeffry Wyatville and erected in 1832 in memory of the third Duke, who is noted as ´the Father of British Inland Navigation`. Its viewing platform reached by 172 steps is open to the public.

    The walk, which is heavily-wooded, first leads you southwards from the Bridgewater Monument along the top of a wooded ridge

to join the Chiltern Way above Aldbury village where there is a fine view. You then turn east and follow the Way towards Ashridge and Little Gaddesden, before leaving the Way and turning northwest to Ringshall and the top of the Chiltern escarpment at Ward's Hurst Farm. From here, you then turn south, entering more woodland and returning to your starting point.

Starting from the end of the road to Bridgewater Monument, take the Hertfordshire Way (bridleway AB20) through the left-hand of two gates and following a macadam drive between the National Trust shop and the Monument. Where its macadam surface ends, take a gravel track straight on into woodland, ignoring a branching path to the left and continuing gently downhill at first, then gradually bearing left and levelling out. Now, at a fork, leaving the Hertfordshire Way, keep left and continue straight on, following the contours of the hillside for over a third of a mile, ignoring a crossing bridleway and passing a seat to your left with a fine view across Aldbury towards Tring and Aylesbury. On reaching a crossing powerline where a clearing to your right offers fine views towards Aldbury Nowers and Pitstone Hill, turn left onto bridleway AB14, **joining the Chiltern Way** and following a stone track. You soon cross a drive by a lodge and take the main track straight on for half a mile, ignoring all branching or crossing paths or tracks to cross the B4506 by a corner of a field to your left onto Berkhamsted Common.

Berkhamsted Common with its extensive woodland is today taken for granted as a place where local people and Londoners can go for fresh air and exercise, but few of its many visitors realise that in 1866 it was all but lost to land enclosure. In that year, 400 acres of the Common, which had, in mediæval times, formed part of the park of Berkhamsted's Norman castle, were enclosed by the lord of the manor, Lord Brownlow of Ashridge Park, with a high iron fence. This might easily have led to the land being split into fields and brought into agricultural use, but Augustus Smith, owner of the nearby Ashlyns Estate and one of the enraged Berkhamsted commoners, supported by Lord Eversley, chairman of the newly-founded Commons Preservation Society (now renamed as the Open Spaces Society), assembled a gang of 100 London labourers and chartered a special train to bring them by dead of night to Berkhamsted Common. By 6 a.m. the fence had been completely dismantled and four years of litigation followed, but finally, in 1870, Augustus Smith won, with an injunction being granted forbidding enclosure and defining the rights of common. The judgment did not, of course, grant public access but preserved the rights of common, so that, when the Law of Property Act 1925 granted public access to urban commons, Berkhamsted Common was able to qualify, subject to certain limitations to protect the golf course.

From the B4506, take bridleway NC46 straight on eastwards for a quarter mile along an avenue of ancient beech and oak trees with a pronounced boundary bank to your left. By the corner of a field to your left, turn left onto path LG5, following the inside edge of the wood. Where the field fence turns away to your right, go straight on, soon wiggling to your right, passing right of a pond and joining a track which merges from your left. On reaching a bend in a macadam private road, join it and follow it straight on, soon crossing the Hertfordshire Way and Prince's Riding, part of the landscaping carried out by Capability Brown in about 1767, where Ashridge House can be seen two-thirds of a mile to your right and the Bridgewater Monument is nearly a mile to your left. On emerging from the woods onto Ashridge Golf Course, keep straight on past Old Park Lodge. Where the macadam surface ends, fork right onto a waymarked path, passing right of a barn and continuing downhill through woodland to emerge onto another part of the golf course. Here keep straight on, passing right of a green and left of the clubhouse, then take a waymarked path through a copse to join a macadam drive and follow it straight on.

After 150 yards, by a three-armed signpost, **leaving the Chiltern Way** and the macadam drive, turn left onto path LG3, crossing the left-hand corner of a raised tee, a golfers'path and a macadam drive by a 20 mph speed limit sign. Here take a grassy track straight on, passing right of a copse and left of an oak tree, then a birch, then a wooden bench to enter a copse. Now keep straight on through the copse, across a fairway and past a sign facing away from you, then continue through a strip of woodland to enter a fenced path between gardens leading to a private road. Cross this road and take the fenced path straight on. On emerging into a scrubby field, continue to follow the left-hand fence, later bearing left to reach a kissing-gate leading to the B4506 on the edge of Ringshall, a hamlet on the edge of the Ashridge Estate straddling the Buckinghamshire boundary.

Turn right onto this road, disregarding Beacon Road to your left, then cross the B4506 and follow its left-hand footway. Now ignore the Little Gaddesden road to your right where you should look out for a castellated former lodge of Ashridge Park to your right, designed by Sir Jeffry Wyatville, who completed Ashridge itself. Opposite a red-brick farm building, turn left through a kissing-gate onto path ED21 (soon becoming IV17), bearing half right across a field to reach a small gate leading to the concrete road to Ringshall Reservoir by a recently-restored cottage. Do **not** join the concrete road, but turn right and follow the right-hand hedge past the

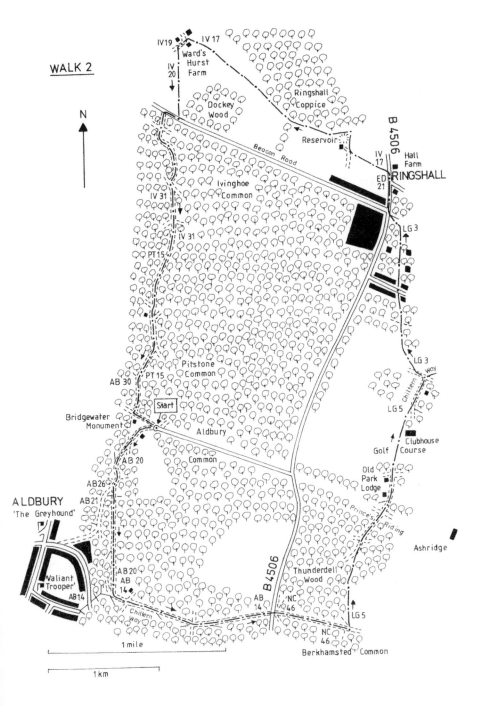

WALK 2

N

IV19
IV 17
Ward's Hurst Farm
IV 20
Dockey Wood
Ringshall Coppice
Beacon Road
Reservoir
B 4506
IV 17
Hall Farm
ED 21
RINGSHALL
Ivinghoe Common
IV 31
LG 3
IV 31
PT 15
Pitstone Common
Chiltern Way
PT 15
AB 30
LG 3
LG 5
Start
Bridgewater Monument
Aldbury Common
Golf Course
Clubhouse
AB 20
Old Park Lodge
AB 26
ALDBURY
'The Greyhound'
AB 21
Prince's Riding
Ashridge
'Valiant Trooper'
AB 14
AB 20
AB 14
B 4506
Thunderdell Wood
AB 14
NC 46
LG 5
Chiltern Way
NC 46
Berkhamsted Common

1 mile

1 km

19

underground reservoir. At the far side of the reservoir, turn left and continue beside its fence to a small gate, then follow the outside edge of a wood called Ringshall Coppice straight on through a field and along a fenced path. Near the far end of the next field, by a large beech tree protruding from the wood, leave the wood edge and keep straight on across the field to cross a stile by a gate under an oak tree. Now continue towards the right-hand end of Ward's Hurst Farm and a wood to the right-hand of two gates in the next hedge, then keep straight on towards an electricity pole right of a green barn to reach a small gate in a further hedge. Do **not** go through this gate, but turn left onto path IV35, following a right-hand hedge through two fields. In the second field, just before an oak tree, by a concealed stile, bear half left onto path IV20, crossing the field to a stile just right of its far corner leading to Beacon Road.

Turn right onto this road, then, after 60 yards, turn left onto an unmarked permissive path into woodland at Ivinghoe Common, following a wide grassy track at first, ignoring a crossing path and a branching path to your right, then bearing left and later right and eventually merging with a wide gravel track (path IV31). Take this track straight on through the woods for two-thirds of a mile (soon becoming path PT15), then, some 150 yards beyond a wooden shed to your right, keep right at a fork, soon crossing a bridge over a sunken way and reentering Hertfordshire, then continuing on bridleway AB30 until you reach the clearing by the Bridgewater Monument where your starting point is to your left.

WALK 3   Little Gaddesden
(Hudnall Common)

Length of Walk: 6.4 miles / 10.3 Km
Starting Point: Small car park on Hudnall Common.
Grid Ref: TL007128
Maps: OS Landranger Sheet 166
           OS Explorer Sheet 182
           Chiltern Society FP Map No.20
How to get there / Parking: Hudnall Common, 5 miles north-west of Hemel Hempstead, may be reached from the town by taking the A4146 towards Leighton Buzzard for over 5 miles passing Great Gaddesden. At the next crossroads turn left into Hudnall Lane, signposted to Little Gaddesden. After two-thirds of a mile, at an unmarked crossroads, turn left, ignoring Pond Lane to your right and continuing for a quarter mile to a small gravel car park on your left where the scrub to your left gives way to open common.
Notes: Heavy nettle growth may be encountered on path ST29 and byway GG5 in the summer months.

Hudnall Common, on the edge of Little Gaddesden with its fine views across the upper Gade valley into Bedfordshire, like much of the land around, is now owned and protected by the National Trust. Little Gaddesden itself, a long straggling village, most of which is on one side of the Ringshall - Nettleden road with Ashridge Park on the other, can boast an attractive village green by which is a timber-framed cottage with an overhanging upper floor called John o'Gaddesden's House, which was reputedly home to this fourteenth-century doctor to Edward II and Edward III, who died in 1361, but is thought more likely to date from the fifteenth century. The stone-built manor house also dates from 1576, while the fifteenth-century parish church, which stands in splendid isolation in fields at the end of a cul-de-sac lane, is principally notable for the wealth of memorials it contains to members of the Egerton family, the Earls and Dukes of Bridgewater, who held nearby Ashridge from 1604 to 1849.

The walk, which explores the upper reaches of the Gade valley and offers fine views in places, first leads you northwestwards

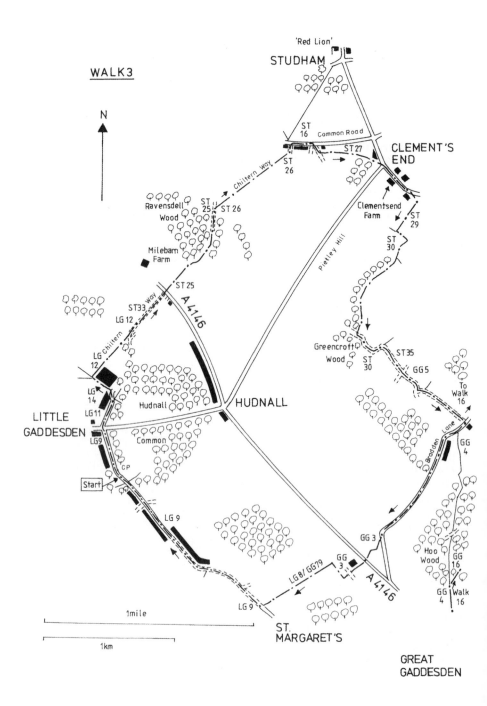

WALK 3

N

'Red Lion'

STUDHAM

ST
16   Common Road

ST 27   CLEMENT'S
END

Chiltern Way

ST
26

Ravensdell   ST   ST 26
Wood   25

Clementsend
Farm   ST
29

Milebam
Farm

Pietley Hill   ST
30

ST 25

ST33 Way   A4146
LG 12   Chiltern

LG Chiltern
12

Greencroft   ST 35
Wood   ST
30   GG 5
To
Walk
16

LG
14

LG11   Hudnall   HUDNALL
LG9   Broadden Lane

LITTLE
GADDESDEN

Common   GG
4

CP

Start

LG 9

GG 3

A4146

LG 8/ GG79   GG   Hoo   GG
3   Wood   16

GG   Walk
4   16

1mile

LG 9

ST.
MARGARET'S

GREAT
GADDESDEN

1km

22

across Hudnall Common to join the Chiltern Way before crossing the Gade valley to the edge of Studham. Leaving the Way, you then turn south through remote country to recross the valley above Great Gaddesden and climb to the edge of St. Margaret's, finally returning along the ridge to Hudnall Common.

Starting from the small car park on Hudnall Common where there are fine views across the Gade valley towards Studham, follow the road (byway LG9) back to the crossroads, then take bridleway LG11 straight on along a cul-de-sac road. After 250 yards, at a right-hand bend, fork left onto path LG14 leading between garden hedges to a kissing-gate, then follow a right-hand hedge straight on to another kissing-gate, where Little Gaddesden Church may be glimpsed through the trees ahead. Now, **joining the Chiltern Way**, turn right through a hedge gap onto path LG12, following a right-hand hedge downhill with fine views opening out across the Gade Valley ahead, eventually passing a copse and reaching a gap in the bottom hedge. Now ignore a bridlegate to your right and rejoin bridleway LG11, following a grassy track straight on downhill beside a right-hand hedge, soon crossing the Bedfordshire boundary and continuing (now on bridleway ST33) to the A4146 in the valley bottom.

Cross this road and take bridleway ST25 straight on, passing through a gap left of a padlocked gate and following a left-hand hedge uphill. Soon after the hedge bears right, pass through a hedge gap, then go straight on uphill between a hedge and a deer fence protecting a young plantation, passing a copse to your right and eventually entering Ravensdell Wood. Keep straight on through this wood to a gate into a field, then follow a grassy track beside a right-hand hedge straight on. After 50 yards, turn right through a kissing-gate onto path ST26 and bear half left across a field, aiming just left of a line of three trees and a cottage with white window frames at Studham beyond and eventually reaching a kissing-gate. Now go straight on, passing left of a lightning-damaged ash tree to reach a kissing-gate by a gate left of the cottage, then follow a short drive to a gate and stile onto Common Road on the edge of Studham.

Studham, the southernmost village in Bedfordshire, nestles in a hollow in the backland of the Dunstable Downs, surrounded by an extensive upland plateau. Until 1897, the village, which was once a centre of the straw-plait industry and was one of the early strongholds of Nonconformity, in fact, straddled the Hertfordshire boundary and it was only then that the southern half of its extensive common and many of its scattered farms and cottages were transferred to the same county as the church and village centre. The cement-rendered thirteenth-century church, which is somewhat isolated and hidden at

23

the end of its cul-de-sac lane, has a surprisingly beautiful interior with fine carved stone capitals and an unusual carved Norman font predating the present building.

Here, **leaving the Chiltern Way**, turn right onto Common Road, then, at a slight left-hand bend just past the entrance to Bury Farm, turn right onto bridleway ST27, following the drive to Oakwood Lodge past a pair of cottages, then forking half left across a field to reach the left-hand corner of a tree belt. Now go straight on through a hedge gap and follow the edge of the tree belt, eventually passing right of some tennis courts to reach a road junction. Here cross the priority road (Pedley Hill) and take Clements End Road straight on towards Gaddesden Row, Flamstead and Redbourn.

Having passed Clements End Farm to your right and rounded a left-hand bend, fork right onto fenced path ST29, following the back of the roadside hedge past farm sheds to a kissing-gate, then bearing half right across a field to a hedge gap by an overgrown kissing-gate. Go through this and bear right following the right-hand hedge. At the far end of the field, go through a hedge gap and turn left onto path ST30, following a left-hand hedge. At a field corner turn right, then ignore the first gap in the left-hand hedge. On nearing a copse, turn left through the second gap in the hedge and continue for a third of a mile, first along the left-hand side of the copse, then beside a right-hand hedge and then along the edge of another copse, gradually bearing left and later winding. Where a grassy track emerges from the copse, turn left onto it, bearing right and passing through a gate, then bearing left and soon left again, following a left-hand hedge to a field corner. Here turn right onto path ST35, still following a left-hand hedge to reach gates in another field corner. Turn left through these, then right through a second set of gates and reentering Hertfordshire, take restricted byway GG5 straight on through a hedge gap, following a grassy track beside a left-hand hedge, soon bearing right. Where the hedge and track bear left, turn sharp left through gates into a green lane and follow it for a quarter mile to reach Bradden Lane opposite Hatches Barn, a good example of a redundant weatherboarded barn converted for residential use.

Turn right into this quiet narrow lane and follow it for nearly two-thirds of a mile, eventually descending into the Gade valley, then, at a sharp left-hand bend, leave the road and take path GG3 straight on through a kissing-gate, bearing slightly left across a field to a footbridge over the upper reaches of the River Gade, which are often dry. Now keep straight on, passing through two further kissing-gates to reach the A4146. Cross this main road carefully and take the continuation of path GG3, passing through a wicket gate left of the gate to The Croft and taking its left-hand drive, following a left-hand hedge, passing left of a barn, then take a fenced grassy track straight on uphill. By the top end of the right-hand field, turn right and follow the right-hand fence within a tree belt, then beside a left-hand hedge to cross a stile where there are fine views up the Gade valley. Now turn left through a hedge gap and take path LG8/GG79, following a left-hand hedge uphill to a gap in the top hedge. Here bear slightly right across a large field, heading for an ash tree and large lightning-damaged sweet chestnut when these come into view ahead, with fine views behind you across the Gade valley, to reach the end of the macadam road at St. Margaret's, named after the former twelfth-century nunnery of St. Margaret de Bosco.

Here, joining the Hertfordshire Way, turn right onto the rough continuation of the road (byway LG9) and follow it for nearly a mile, with wide views to your left in places at first towards woodland on the Ashridge Estate and Little Gaddesden, then leaving the Hertfordshire Way (which turns left), becoming enclosed and with its macadam surface resuming, eventually reaching Hudnall Common and your starting point.

WALK 4   Dunstable Downs

Length of Walk: 8.6 miles / 13.8 Km
Starting Point: Junction of B4541 and Isle of Wight Lane on Dunstable Downs (Robertson Corner).
Grid Ref: TL009197
Maps: OS Landranger Sheet 166
OS Explorer Sheets 182 & 193
Chiltern Society FP Map No.21
How to get there / Parking: Dunstable Downs car park, 1.5 miles south of the town centre, may be reached from it by taking the B489 towards Aston Clinton, then turning left onto the B4541 towards The Downs and Whipsnade. At the top of the hill, park in one of the right-hand car parks.

The Dunstable Downs, with their spectacular views along the Chilterns to Ivinghoe Beacon and out over the Vale of Aylesbury towards Oxfordshire and the Cotswolds, are today a real ´honey-pot´ for people from Dunstable, Luton and farther afield, for picnics and walks with superb views and ample parking. Four thousand years ago, these hills must also have been frequented, as, at the northern end of the Downs, are the Five Knolls, five huge Neolithic or Bronze Age barrows, where excavations have not only revealed remains from this period, but also a large number of skeletons originating from the fifth century A.D., some of whom had injured bones or their hands tied behind their backs, suggesting that they were the victims of some battle or massacre.

The walk first leads you from the Dunstable Downs around the rim of Kensworth Quarry, the largest (and possibly last) active chalk quarry in the Chilterns, before turning south across a quiet upland plateau passing the remote churches of Kensworth and Studham. Joining the Chiltern Way, you then turn north by way of Whipsnade with its large open common to reach the top of the escarpment at Whipsnade Down and follow it back with superb views to your starting point.

Starting from the junction of the B4541 and Isle of Wight Lane at Dunstable Downs known as Robertson Corner, take the B4541 towards Dunstable, then turn immediately right onto the right-hand of two paths (KN18), a path with a fence to your left and mature beech trees to your right, to reach the corner of woodland. Here go straight on through a squeeze-stile by a padlocked gate into the woodland, soon ignoring a branching path to your right and later bearing right. Where the waymarked path turns left, leave it and take a permissive path straight on to gates in the fence of Kensworth Quarry, then turn left and follow the quarry fence for two-thirds of a mile with wide views across this vast chalk quarry in places, eventually joining path KN7. (NB If the permissive path is closed, an alternative route via definitive paths KN18, D28, D27 and KN7 is shown on the plan).

On emerging into a field, where fine views gradually open out to your left across Dunstable towards Blows Down and Luton beyond, follow the right-hand hedge concealing the quarry fence straight on through two fields with the hedge petering out to reveal the fence again in the second field. At the far end of this field, take a wide grassy track straight on between a strip of woodland and the quarry fence, ignoring branching tracks through the trees and passing the end of the quarry. Where the quarry fence turns right, take a grassy track straight on through woodland, then, at a T-junction of tracks, turn sharp left onto path KN19 along a short green lane. On entering a field, turn right onto path KN4, following the right-hand hedge at first. After 90 yards, where the hedge bears slightly right, bear slightly left across the field to a stile into Kensworth churchyard. Now bear slightly left, passing just right of the church, dating from about 1120 but with a fifteenth-century tower, to reach gates, then bear slightly right to a road junction.

Kensworth, which most people only know as a straggling village of apparently fairly modern origin stretched out along a mile and a half of the B4540 and Common Road at Kensworth Common, gives the impression of being a typical ´closed village`, where early land inclosure prevented the poorer villagers from living in the original settlement, in this case Church End with its ancient church and large farms or the equally old hamlet of Kensworth Lynch to the east, and were forced instead to encroach on what had always been a remote upland common, before the creation of Whipsnade Wild Animal Park in 1931 and the construction of a wide modern road leading to it. The distance between the largest settlement in the parish and the parish church may also explain why in the 1660s Kensworth became a stronghold of Nonconformity and it was at Kensworth Common rather than Church End where the Non-conformist chapels were later built.

Now take Hollick's Lane straight on uphill. At the top, just before an electricity pylon, turn left through a hedge gap onto the continuation of path KN4, bearing half right across a field, heading just left of a lightning-damaged beech tree to reach a marker post at a kink in a field boundary. Now keep straight on across two fields, passing just left of a chestnut tree in the valley bottom to reach the corner of a tree belt. Here bear slightly right into a green lane and follow it uphill to the B4540 at Kensworth Common.

Turn left onto this road and follow it for 250 yards passing a mini-roundabout, then turn right through a squeeze-stile beside a white gate and take path KN3 along the drive towards Gate House and Blake Hall. Just past Gate House to your left, fork right into a hedged path parallel to the drive, near Blake Hall bearing right through a hedge gap into a field. Now on path KN14, follow the left-hand hedge, soon entering another hedged path, later with a fence to your left. On emerging by the gates to a sawmill, take its drive straight on to a bend in Dovehouse Lane. Bear slightly left onto this road and follow it for a third of a mile passing Shortgrove Manor Farm to reach a T-junction.

Here turn right into Buckwood Lane, then, after 50 yards, turn left onto path ST4, passing a redundant stile and entering woodland. At a three-way fork, bear left, following the inside edge of the wood uphill, soon with an enclosing hedge to your right. Now ignore a branching fenced path to your right and eventually emerge by a corner of a garden fence into the left-hand field. Here follow a right-hand hedge and later fences straight on, soon with woodland to your left. Now keep straight on, ignoring branching paths into the woodland to your left and the end of a residential road at Holywell to your right. At the far side of the wood, bear half left along a fenced path between fields to enter another wood. Now take an obvious path straight on, eventually becoming enclosed by fences and descending to Dunstable Road on the edge of Studham, where you turn left.

Studham, the southernmost village in Bedfordshire, nestles in a hollow surrounded by an extensive upland plateau. Until 1897, the village, which, like Kensworth, was once a centre of the straw-plait industry and an early stronghold of Nonconformity, in fact, straddled the Hertfordshire boundary and it was only then that the southern half of its extensive common and many of its scattered farms and cottages were transferred to the same county as the church and village centre. The cement-rendered thirteenth-century church, which is somewhat isolated and hidden at the end of its cul-de-sac lane, has a surprisingly beautiful interior with fine carved stone capitals and an unusual carved Norman font predating the present building.

After 100 yards, turn right through a kissing-gate between field gates onto path ST3, following a right-hand hedge through two fields. At the far side of the second field, turn right onto path ST18, following a grassy track beside a left-hand hedge. On entering a second field, now on path ST19, bear half right, still following the track to the right-hand corner of the churchyard, then bear slightly left. At a T-junction of tracks in a field corner, take path ST21 straight on through a kissing-gate, passing large ash and oak trees and continuing to a kissing-gate and footbridge into Church Grove.

Inside this wood, **joining the Chiltern Way**, turn right onto bridleway ST6, following the inside edge of the wood and ignoring a branching path to your left. On emerging from the wood into a field corner, ignore a branching track to your right and take a grassy track beside a right-hand hedge straight on through two fields. At the far end of the second field, go straight on into a copse, then, at a fork, take the right-hand option straight on, soon reaching the perimeter fence of Whipsnade Zoo. Now keep straight on between this fence and a tree belt for over a quarter mile to reach Studham Lane. Turn left into this narrow road closed to vehicular traffic and follow it for a quarter mile. Where the lane forks, keep right, then immediately turn right through a kissing-gate onto path ST10, following a left-hand hedge to pass through a kissing-gate at the far side of the field. Now turn left through gates onto path WP8 and follow a right-hand hedge towards Whipsnade Church. At the far side of the field, go through a kissing-gate into the churchyard and pass left of the church to reach gates leading out to Whipsnade Green.

Whipsnade is notable for its extensive green, around which its scattered cottages are situated, and being the highest village in Bedfordshire. Its unusual brick-built church has a sixteenth-century tower and an eighteenth-century nave but incorporates details of an earlier building, while at the back of the village is the Tree Cathedral planted in the 1930s by Edmund Kell Blyth in memory of friends killed in the First World War and now looked after by the National Trust. However, what Whipsnade is best known for is the Zoo, which was opened by the Royal Zoological Society in 1931 to exhibit and breed its hardier animals in natural surroundings. The Zoo in its scenically spectacular setting can be toured by a steam railway which you may have heard while skirting its perimeter.

At the church gates, turn left and follow the back of the green at first. Having crossed the drive to Church Farm, keep straight on to a road junction left of a former chapel. Here cross the B4540 and take the road signposted to the ´Tree Cathedral`. At a fork, keep right, then immediately bear right again through a gap by a padlocked gate onto bridleway WP4, following a green lane past the Tree Cathedral and Whipsnade Jubilee Orchard. On reaching a gate into the Tree

Cathedral to your left, bear right to pass through a fence gap onto a private road.

Turn left onto this road, then, after 70 yards, fork right, following a right-hand fence through scrubland, part of the Sallow Springs Nature Reserve, then along the edge of two meadows. At the far end of the second meadow, turn left and follow a right-hand fence to rejoin the private road. Turn right onto this, ignoring a branching path to your left and the entrance to a luxury housing development to your right and soon entering Sallowspring Wood. At the far side of the wood, by a telecommunications mast, fork right, joining bridleway WP1 which follows a gravel lane along the edge of the wood. On emerging onto another private road, take a sunken way straight on along the edge of the wood to reach a bridlegate leading to Whipsnade Down, where superb panoramic views open out with a glider airfield below you, Dunstable Downs to your right, Totternhoe Knolls ahead and the Vale of Aylesbury beyond. Here turn right onto a National Trust permissive bridleway, following the top hedge of the Down for 250 yards to reach a bridlegate. Go through this, then follow a right-hand hedge straight on through scrubland, then across open downland. Where the hedge ends, **leaving the Chiltern Way**, bear slightly right, passing left of a large iron sculpture, crossing a macadam path and heading for tall trees on the skyline to reach your starting point.

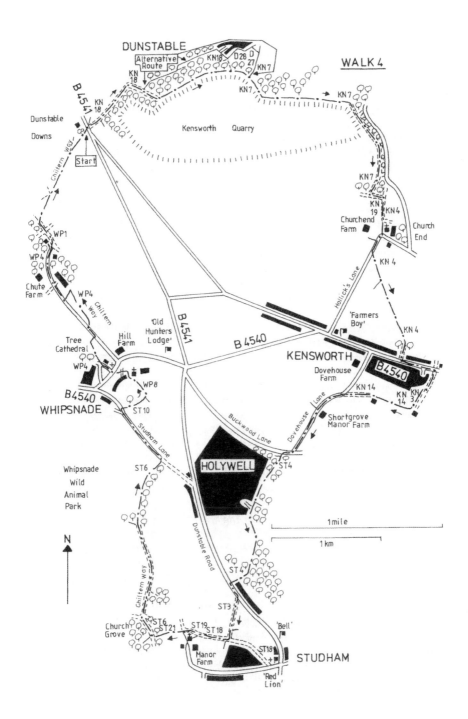

DUNSTABLE

Alternative Route

KN18 KN18 D28 D27 KN7

WALK 4

KN 18

B 4541

KN 18

Dunstable Downs

Start

Chiltern Way

Kensworth   Quarry

KN7

KN 7

KN 7

KN 7

KN 19   KN4

Churchend Farm

Church End

WP1

WP4

Chute Farm

WP4

Chiltern Way

Old Hunters Lodge'

B 4541

Hollick's Lane

'Farmers Boy'

KN 4

KN 4

Tree Cathedral

Hill Farm

WP4

B 4540

KENSWORTH

B4540

WP8

B 4540

WHIPSNADE

ST 10

Dovehouse Farm

KN 14

KN 14

KN 3

Studham Lane

Buckwood Lane

Dovehouse Lane

Shortgrove Manor Farm

Whipsnade Wild Animal Park

ST6

HOLYWELL

ST4

ST4

N

1 mile

1 km

Dunstable Road

Chiltern Way

ST4

ST3

ST6

ST19

Church Grove

ST21

ST18

'Bell'

ST18

Manor Farm

STUDHAM

'Red Lion'

31

WALK 5   Houghton Regis

Length of Walk: 9.2 miles / 14.9 Km
Starting Point: Houghton Regis Church/´Kings Arms`.
Grid Ref: TL018239
Maps: OS Landranger Sheet 166
OS Explorer Sheets 192 & 193
Chiltern Society FP Map No.23
Parking: From the traffic lights by the church at the junction of the A5120 and Houghton Regis High Street, take the High Street towards Luton and park in front of the church or turn right at the next roundabout for a larger car park.
Notes: Paths HR17 & HR45 may be diverted due to a proposed housing development near Bidwell and path HRa11 will be affected when the Dunstable Northern Bypass is built. Heavy nettle growth may be encountered in various places in the summer months.

Houghton Regis, on a Chiltern foothill, with its fine fourteenth-century church with a fifteenth-century tower and clerestory and a Norman font, its large green and some thatched cottages, must once have been picturesque, but, since the 1960s, it has been swamped with modern housing and commercial development, making its character suburban. The name Houghton Regis is of Saxon origin, its first part meaning ´settlement on a hill' and its second denoting a royal manor and it was this which both saved it from being sacked when visited by William the Conqueror soon after the Battle of Hastings and caused nearby Dunstable (then part of the manor) to be chosen as the site for Henry I's palace and priory, of which Dunstable's present magnificent church was only a small part. More recently the chalk, on which the village is built, brought it renewed prosperity, as the straw-plait made from the white straw which grew on it, was valuable to Luton's straw-hat industry, while the chalk itself was quarried for making cement.

    This walk, which abounds in fine views, explores the Chiltern foothills around the upper reaches of Ouzel Brook, crossing the valley to Wingfield on another low ridge with panoramic views. It then turns southwestwards along the ridge, leading you over a hilltop above Tilsworth with more panoramic views, before descending into the village and continuing across the valley to the

foot of Totternhoe Knolls. You then follow an old railway line to the picturesque hamlet of Sewell where you join the Chiltern Way and follow it back to Houghton Regis.

Starting from the traffic lights by Houghton Regis Church and the ´Kings Arms`, take the High Street towards Luton past the church. Now turn left onto path HR18, following the churchyard wall past a shopping centre, then bearing right then left to reach the end of Angels Lane. Here take a fenced permissive path straight on to the end of All Saints Road, then continue along this road to a T-junction. Now turn right into Churchfield Road, then immediately left onto another permissive path leading to Dellmont Road. Turn right onto this, then immediately left onto path HR17 along the edge of a narrow green to rejoin Churchfield Road. Here turn right, then left into Dell Road. At its end, take the continuation of path HR17 straight on through a fence gap into a copse, then immediately fork right, following a left-hand fence downhill through the copse into a field. Here bear slightly left, heading for the right-hand-most pylon in a distant powerline to reach the left-hand end of an old iron-railing fence on a low ridge.

Now, **joining the Chiltern Way**, take path HR45, bearing slightly right to the corner of a fence, then follow this fence straight on to a kissing-gate. Here go straight on, following a left-hand hedge at first. Where the hedge turns left, bear slightly right across the field to pass through a gap in the corner of a hedge and follow the left-hand field boundary to the far end of the field. Here cross a footbridge and stile, then, **leaving the Chiltern Way**, take path HRa11 straight on across the next field to a stile in the far corner leading to the entrance to a drive off the A5120. Cross this drive and a second stile opposite, then follow the back of the main road hedge straight on through two fields. On crossing a stile into a third field, follow the field edge straight on beside the A5120, ignoring a crossing bridleway and continuing until the roadside hedge resumes. Here turn left, crossing the main road and take bridleway HR15 opposite, passing through a gap by a gate and following a track beside a right-hand hedge straight on with fine views to your left towards Houghton Regis and Dunstable and ahead towards the old quarry face at Chalk Hill and Totternhoe Knolls. After 250 yards, turn right over a footbridge onto path CG19, following a left-hand hedge uphill with more fine views towards the Dunstable Downs, Totternhoe Knolls and Ivinghoe Beacon beyond to your left and Houghton Regis and Dunstable behind you. Where the left-hand hedge ends, cross a footbridge and bear half right across the field to a hedge gap, then bear slightly left and take a fenced path beside a right-hand hedge to a squeeze-stile onto Tebworth Road, Wingfield, virtually opposite the ´Plough Inn`.

Wingfield, a hilltop hamlet of Chalgrave parish, whose mother village is a ´lost village` consisting of a church and a farm, apart from its thatched pub, has little of interest except Pond Farm, a timber-framed brick building dating from 1699, but what it may lack in historical interest is more than compensated by the fine views which are available at various points around the village.

Turn left onto this road and follow it through Wingfield. After a third of a mile, at a sharp right-hand bend just past a bungalow called Lark Rise, fork left over a stile by a gate onto path CG14, turning right onto a concrete farm road with superb panoramic views towards Houghton Regis, Dunstable, Totternhoe Knolls, the Dunstable Downs and Ivinghoe Beacon, soon crossing a stile by a gate. Where the concrete road ends at a second gate and stile, take a fenced grassy track straight on beside a right-hand hedge to cross a stile by gates. Now follow a right-hand hedge straight on through the next field ignoring the stile of a branching path. At the far end of the field, cross a stile by a gate and keep straight on across the next field, eventually joining and following the right-hand side of a ditch. At the far side of the field, keep right of a hedge and follow it to cross a footbridge, then cross a farm road and take a fenced path straight on beside a left-hand hedge, eventually bearing right. Now ignore a kissing-gate in the fence and turn left through a bollarded hedge gap to reach the A5 on the course of the Roman road known as Watling Street near the Little Chef.

Turn right onto its footway. After 50 yards, turn left, crossing the A5 and take bridleway HK-TW8 through a gate and bridlegate, then follow a left-hand hedge and ditch through two fields. Near the far end of the second field, turn left over a gated culvert and take path TW7, bearing half right across a field to a gated culvert in the far corner. Now bear half right across the next field to cross a stile and footbridge in the far hedge between the third and fourth electricity poles onto a golf course, then turn right, following the right-hand hedge uphill along its edge to pass through a gap in the top hedge. Here bear half left across the golf course, passing right of a green and a bunker. At the crest of the ridge, where superb views open out ahead across Tilsworth towards Totternhoe Knolls and the Dunstable Downs, aim just right of a pond and green to cross a stile in the bottom corner of the golf course. Now bear left across the corner of a field to enter a fenced path by a pond. Here turn right onto fenced path TW14, eventually emerging into the back of the garden of the ´Anchor` pub. Now go straight on through the garden to the corner of a fence, then follow a left-hand fence straight on to reach a gate leading to Dunstable Road, Tilsworth.

Tilsworth, facing the Chilterns on its hillside above the valley of Ouzel Brook, though somewhat spoilt by nondescript modern housing, can boast a mediæval timber-framed brick barn and a moated manor house with a fifteenth-century ironstone gatehouse, while its thirteenth-century church contains the fine canopied tombs of Gabriel Fowler who died in 1582 and Sir Henry Chester who died in 1666. In the churchyard is the tomb of ´Female unknown`, who was found in 1821 propped against a tree in Blackgrove Wood with her throat cut.

Cross Dunstable Road and turn right onto its footway passing the ´Anchor` and a small green, then continue along Stanbridge Road towards the church. At a right-hand bend by a bus shelter, turn left onto fenced path TW1, which leads you between gardens to a kissing-gate into a field where fine views open out ahead towards Totternhoe Knolls and the Dunstable Downs beyond. Go straight on across this field, heading just left of a distant pylon to a kissing-gate in the next hedge, then bear half right across the next field, heading just left of another pylon behind Stanbridge Wood to cross a footbridge and stile in the right-hand hedge. Now bear half left across another field to cross a stile and footbridge by the left-hand corner of the wood, then follow the outside edge of Blackgrove Wood straight on to its far end. Here, just past a twin-poled pylon by the corner of a hedge, turn left onto path TW2, crossing the field to the right-hand of two small trees left of the powerline. Now turn right and follow a left-hand ditch past a large pylon until you reach a culvert across the ditch where the ditch bears left. Turn left over this culvert and then right, following the field edge to reach the A505 fence by a second culvert. Here turn right, crossing the culvert and taking path TT23, passing through two squeeze-stiles flanking a field entrance and following the A505 fence for a third of a mile. Soon after a hedge supplements the fence, turn left through a squeeze-stile, over a culvert and up a flight of steps to the A505.

Cross this fast road carefully, then descend steps opposite and continue over a footbridge, through a squeeze-stile and over a culvert into a field. Here bear slightly right to a hedge gap left of two twin-poled pylons leading to the course of the former Dunstable Branch of the London & North Western Railway, built in 1859 and closed in 1962, now part of cycle track NCN6. Turn left onto the old railway and follow it for one mile, climbing gently onto a tree-lined embankment. On approaching the bridge over Sewell Lane, where Sewell Farm can be seen through the trees to your left, fork right down a slope to reach a junction of lanes by the bridge.

Here turn left, **joining the Chiltern Way** and Icknield Way, taking Sewell Lane under the bridge. Now follow this road through the picturesque hamlet of Sewell for nearly a quarter mile. Just past the drive to Sewell Manor, turn left through a squeeze-stile onto path HR24, following a fenced path downhill, then bearing right, eventually crossing a stile into a field. Bear slightly left across this field to cross a stile under a tall sycamore tree, then turn left onto a sometimes overgrown path through a tree belt, eventually emerging over a footbridge into a field. Now turn right and follow this ditch and a sporadic hedge until you reach a tree belt covering the embankment of the A5. Here turn right onto path HR31, following the edge of the tree belt until a marker post indicates a hedge gap leading to a steep flight of steps up the embankment to a stile onto the A5 at Chalk Hill.

Chalk Hill, on the A5 just northwest of Dunstable, must have once been a very steep and dangerous hill for stagecoaches to negotiate, no doubt exacerbated by the slippery nature of chalk surfaces in wet weather, as, in 1837, just before the dawning railway age ruined the financial viability of the turnpikes, the responsible turnpike trust went to the considerable expense of excavating a cutting and creating an embankment to reduce its gradient and produce the long gradual incline we know today.

Cross the A5 carefully and turn right onto its footway, passing a filling station. Just before the ´White Lion` inn, by a traffic island, turn left onto the continuation of path HR31, descending a flight of steps to the old road. Turn left onto this, then, just past a timber-framed cottage, turn right onto an enclosed path (still HR31) and follow it to enter a field. Now follow its left-hand hedge straight on for half a mile, passing Houghton Regis Sewage Works to your left and eventually reaching the corner of a copse concealing an old chalkpit. Here go straight on, passing left of a small fenced compound, entering a green lane and continuing for a quarter mile until you reach a concrete road. **Leaving the Chiltern Way**, cross the concrete road, bearing slightly right onto path HR3, passing left of a concrete fence post, then bearing right and taking a fenced path uphill through scrub to a kissing-gate into a field. Now follow a left-hand hedge straight on uphill, ignoring branching paths into a housing estate. At the far side of the field, keep straight on past the end of an estate road and take a macadamed path straight on through a squeeze-stile for 200 yards. Where the path bears right, turn left onto crossing path HR8, passing the end of a road and continuing to a road junction. Here go straight on, then, after 35 yards, turn left onto crossing path HR6. After 30 yards, turn right onto path HR7, an alleyway leading to the A5120, where you turn right for your starting point.

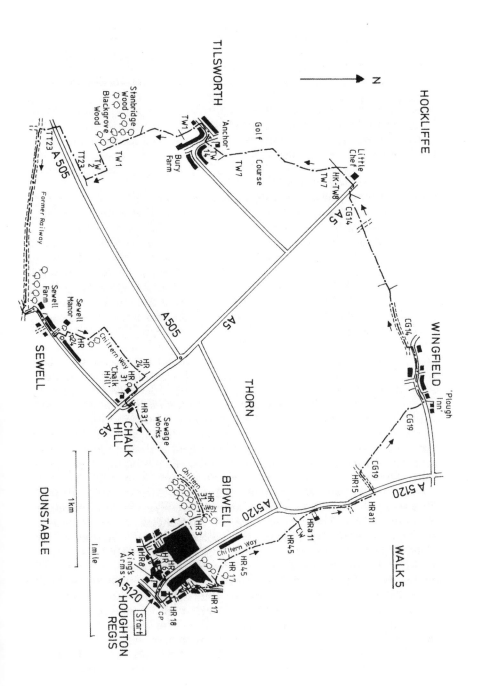

N

HOCKLIFFE

TILSWORTH

Stanbridge Wood
Blackgrove Wood

'Anchor'
Bury Farm

Golf Course

TT23
A 505

Former Railway

Sewell Farm
Sewell Manor

SEWELL

DUNSTABLE

1km

1mile

Tw1
Tw14
Tw1 2
Tw7

Little Chef

HK-Tw8

CG14
A5

A5

THORN

A505

Chiltern Way
'Chalk Hill'
HR 24
HR 31

CHALK HILL

HR31

Sewage Works

Chiltern Way
HR 31
HR 3

BIDWELL

A5120

'King's Arms'
HR8
HR6
CP
HR18
HR17

Chiltern Way
HR 45
HR 17

CW
HRa 11
HR45
HR15
CG19

A5120

'Plough Inn'

WINGFIELD

CG14
CG19

WALK 5

A5120
HOUGHTON REGIS

Start

WALK 6   Sundon Hills

Length of Walk: 5.5 miles / 8.9 Km
Starting Point: Sundon Hills Country Park car park.
Grid Ref: TL047285
Maps: OS Landranger Sheet 166
            OS Explorer Sheet 193
            Chiltern Society FP Maps Nos. 23 & 25
How to get there / Parking: Sundon Hills Country Park, 5.5
    miles northwest of the centre of Luton, may be reached by
    leaving the M1 at Junction 12 (Toddington) and taking the
    A5120 towards Ampthill for half a mile, then turning right
    onto a road signposted to Harlington Station. In Harlington,
    continue past the station to the village crossroads, then turn
    right onto the Sundon road and follow it for 2 miles. On
    nearing the top of a steep hill, turn left into the Sundon Hills
    Country Park car park.

Sundon Hills Country Park with its chalk downland rich in flora
and superb views towards Sharpenhoe Clappers and across the
Bedfordshire lowlands to the north is today a justifiably popular
destination for visitors from nearby towns, to which public access
was gained only thanks to its purchase by the former Bedfordshire
County Council. In the seventeenth century, the surrounding
countryside was, however, the scene of critical events in the life of
John Bunyan, who was arrested at Lower Samshill in 1660.
Bunyan subsequently appeared before the magistrate, Francis
Wingate at his sixteenth-century manor house in Harlington before
being incarcerated for twelve years in Bedford Gaol where he
wrote his ´Pilgrim's Progress`, for which he is still famous today.
Indeed, it is thought that these hills and the Barton Hills to the east
were the inspiration for his reference there to ´the Delectable
Mountains` and this is why they form part of the John Bunyan Trail,
with which a nearby section of the Chiltern Way coincides.
Sundon's large thirteenth-century church with its mediæval murals
and stone seats around its walls for the elderly and infirm from
before the introduction of pews (from which the phrase ´the weak
go to the wall´ derives) was also the setting of the wedding of
William Foster, another of Bunyan's persecutors and Anne
Wingate, the magistrate's sister.

The walk, which is characterised by superb views from and along the Chiltern escarpment, first takes the Chiltern Way from the Sundon Hills Country Park to near Sharpenhoe Clappers, before descending the side of the Clappers and following the foot of this spectacularly steep section of the escarpment westwards to near Harlington. You then climb to rejoin the Chiltern Way west of the country park and return with more fine views to your starting point.

Starting from the entrance to Sundon Hills Country Park car park, **take the Chiltern Way**, bearing slightly left across the car park to pass just right of a red dog-waste bin, then bear right to a kissing-gate. Now bear slightly right, following the top hedge of this large downland field with fine views ahead towards Sharpenhoe Clappers and to your left across the Bedfordshire lowlands. At the far end of the field, go through a kissing-gate, then bear right onto a grassy track, following a right-hand fence round the rim of a steep-sided coombe, then uphill and bearing right. Now fork right through a kissing-gate onto path SU19, following a left-hand hedge gently uphill with fine views behind you. At the far side of the field, turn left through a hedge gap onto path SU4, following the outside edge of Holt Wood straight on, then, at the far end of the wood, bear half left onto a farm track leading to a corner of Fernhill Wood.

Here bear half left again with fine views ahead towards Harlington. At the next corner of this wood, turn right, leaving the track, and follow the outside edge of the wood to the far side of the field. Here ignore a path into the wood and turn left, still following the outside edge of the wood. After 120 yards, by a marker post, you finally enter the wood and bear left to reach a waymarked junction at the top of some steps. Here turn right onto path SL15 and follow it straight on for 350 yards, ignoring branching paths to right and left and soon skirting the top edge of a deep coombe. At a fork, where gates can be seen to your right, fork right towards the gates, then, by the gates, fork left onto a fenced track along the outside edge of the wood. Where this track bears right, leave it and go straight on through a kissing-gate by a gate. Now, diverging from the wood edge, keep straight on across the field with fine views opening out ahead towards Sharpenhoe, Pulloxhill and Ampthill beyond and later to your left towards Harlington, to reach a kissing-gate in the far hedge. Go through this and descend some steps leading down to Sharpenhoe Road opposite the entrance to Sharpenhoe Clappers car park.

The name Sharpenhoe Clappers is of mixed origin, as the village name of Sharpenhoe is Saxon, meaning ´sharp spur of land`, while Clappers comes from Norman French meaning ´rabbit warren`. While the village at the foot of the hill, which unusually has always been a hamlet of the hilltop village of Streatley, may therefore have originated in Saxon times, the hill shows much earlier signs of habitation, as it is capped by an Iron Age hill fort and both Iron Age and Roman pottery have been found there, but the Normans adapted it for breeding rabbits and thus arose the second part of its name. Clappers Wood within the earthworks, though ancient in appearance, was, in fact, only planted between 1834 and 1844 and a painting from 1815 shows it completely bare. In the wood is an obelisk erected by W.A. Robertson in memory of his two brothers who were killed in the First World War and this was also his reason for donating the Clappers to the National Trust in 1939. The former moated manor near Bury Farm just north of the village below was home to both the leading seventeenth-century mathematician, Edmund Wingate and Thomas Norton (1532 - 1584), the Calvinist zealot, who was both Solicitor General to Elizabeth I, nicknamed ´Rackmaster General` due to his ready use of torture against Roman Catholics, and a poet and playwright credited with being the forerunner of and model for Shakespeare and Marlowe.

Cross Sharpenhoe Road and take path SL14 straight on through the car park and a gap by a gate, then along a macadamed track. After 40 yards, on reaching further gates, **leaving the Chiltern Way**, turn left onto fenced bridleway SL42. By the corner of woodland, keep left at a fork, then follow a sunken way steeply downhill. At the bottom, ignore a gate to your right and take the fenced bridleway straight on along the edge of scrubland and later beside a left-hand hedge with fine views ahead towards Sharpenhoe and Pulloxhill and a close-up view of Sharpenhoe Clappers to your right. On reaching a kissing-gate, turn left through a hedge gap onto Sharpenhoe Road and take bridleway SL38 through a gate and gap opposite, following a grassy track beside a left-hand hedge with fine views towards the Sundon Hills and Toddington ahead and Harlington to your right. After over a third of a mile, at a fork by the corner of a fenced meadow, bear slightly left onto fenced path SL15, following the edge of scrubby woodland. On reaching the foot of a steep coombe, of which you previously followed the top edge, turn right, still with the fence to your right and woodland to your left, eventually reaching a crossways.

Here ignore the crossing path and bear half right onto a permissive path waymarked with a butterfly, continuing to follow a fenced route along the edge of the wood with fine views to your right towards Harlington, Pulloxhill and Sharpenhoe. (NB If the permissive should be closed, turn right through a kissing-gate onto path HA25 and take the alternative route via path HA25 and bridleway HA27 shown on

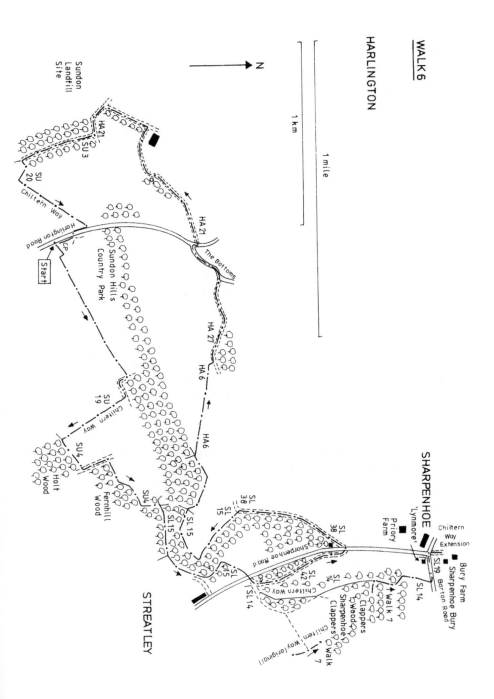

WALK 6

HARLINGTON

41

the plan). After 350 yards, turn right through a small gate onto path HA6 and bear half left across a large field, heading for the left-hand end of a copse with panoramic views towards the Sundon Hills to your left, Harlington ahead and Sharpenhoe Clappers to your right, to reach a concealed hedge gap. Go through this and turn left onto bridleway HA27, following a winding farm track to a bend in a road called The Bottoms.

Turn left onto this road, then, at a T-junction, turn right onto the road to Harlington, immediately turning left at a left-hand bend through a hedge gap onto bridleway HA21. Now take a grassy track beside a left-hand hedge, eventually passing a pond. Just past the pond, bear left through a hedge gap, then bear right and follow a grassy track beside a right-hand hedge at first, then continuing past farm buildings to reach a track junction. Here turn left and follow a grassy track along the right-hand side of a tree belt. At the far end of the tree belt, turn left (still on bridleway HA21) and take a grassy track beside the hedge of Sundon Landfill Site. On reaching the edge of scrubland, follow the track bearing left. After a further 100 yards, turn right onto bridleway SU3, entering the scrubland and following an obvious track gently uphill. On leaving the scrubland, **rejoining the Chiltern Way**, turn left onto path SU20, following the edge of the scrub to a hedge gap in the field corner, where fine views open out ahead towards Harlington and Ampthill beyond. Here turn right and follow the hedge uphill to a field corner, then turn left beside the top hedge with superb views across Bedfordshire to your left, now including Toddington over your left shoulder. At the far side of the field, go straight on through a kissing-gate frame by a padlocked gate onto Harlington Road, where you turn right, then, after 50 yards, turn left through a kissing-gate into the Sundon Hills Country Park, where the car park is to your right.

WALK 7   Barton-le-Clay

Length of Walk: 8.7 miles / 14.0 Km
Starting Point: Junction of B655 (Hexton Road) & Old Road,
Barton-le-Clay.
Grid Ref: TL082306
Maps: OS Landranger Sheet 166
OS Explorer Sheet 193
Chiltern Society FP Map No.25
How to get there / Parking: Barton-le-Clay, 6 miles north of
Luton, may be reached from the town by taking the A6
towards Bedford. After about 5 miles, fork left onto the
B655 towards Hitchin. On reaching the village, turn right
(still on the B655), then, after 200 yards at a sharp left-hand
bend, fork right into Old Road and look for a suitable
on-street parking place.
Notes: Path BC11 may be heavy-going during or after wet
weather. In such conditions, you may prefer to turn right at
Sharpenhoe onto Barton Road and follow it to rejoin the
walk route by the ´Royal Oak` in Barton-le-Clay. Heavy
nettle growth may also be encountered on path BC11 in the
summer months.

Barton-le-Clay, formerly known as Barton-in-the-Clay meaning
´barley farm in the clay land`, sits astride the old route of the A6
from London to Bedford and Carlisle at the foot of the Chiltern
escarpment where the clay land to the north, from which its name
derives, gives way to Chiltern chalk. As such, in the days of the
stagecoach, Barton was a place of busy coaching inns, but earlier
its history was marked by less peaceful pursuits as in 54BC the
nearby 22-acre Iron Age hill fort of Cassivellaunus, dating from
about 550BC and now called Ravensburgh Castle, was attacked by
Julius Cæsar, while the village itself was the scene of a ninth-
century battle between Saxons and Danes. Despite Barton being
swamped by modern housing since World War II, the vicinity of its
church with its picturesque cottages remains an area of rural
tranquillity and beauty. The church itself dates from 1180, but was
much enlarged in the thirteenth century, while its tower is of
fifteenth-century origin and it can also boast a finely-carved roof
depicting eagles, saints and apostles. Its moated timber-framed

rectory dates from about 1550 and is said to be the second oldest parsonage in England still serving its original purpose. It is also said to be haunted by ´a beautiful grey lady` called Anne Humphreys, the wife of the then rector, who is believed to have died in childbirth in 1700 and is said to be searching for her lost love following her husband's subsequent remarriage.

For the walker, Barton's principal attraction is as a centre for walks with spectacular views of and from the range of hills which bears its name and forms the northern-most ridge in the Chilterns and these hills are thought to have been the inspiration for John Bunyan's ´delectable mountains` in his ´Pilgrim's Progress`. This walk, which abounds in superb views, takes advantage of the parallel sections of the original Chiltern Way and Chiltern Way Extension east of their fork at Sharpenhoe Clappers to form a circular route almost entirely using one or other route of the Way. It first takes the Chiltern Way Extension from Barton-le-Clay uphill through the Barton Hills Nature Reserve with its panoramic views to the plateau above, where you transfer to the original Chiltern Way. You then follow this westwards to Streatley before rejoining the crown of the ridge with more fine views and reaching the fork at Sharpenhoe Clappers. Here you take the Chiltern Way Extension again, dropping to Sharpenhoe and continuing across the flat land with views of the escarpment from below to return to Barton-le-Clay.

Starting from the junction of the B655 (Hexton Road) and Old Road, **take the Chiltern Way Extension** straight on along Old Road, so named as it formed part of the ancient London road before its rerouting in 1832 to lessen the gradient of Barton Hill. Just past its junction with Washbrook Close, turn left through gates onto path BC4 across a recreation ground, heading just right of the church and tennis courts to reach a kissing-gate. Now take a macadamed alley to Church Road opposite the church. Here turn right, passing the rectory to your left. After 100 yards, near the end of the lane, turn left onto fenced bridleway BC26, following a left-hand hedge past paddocks and an arable field. By an iron gate, bear right to a fork. Here ignore a green lane to your left and take a permissive path straight on up steps and through a kissing-gate into the Barton Hills Nature Reserve. Traditionally glebe land with customary public access, the Barton Hills in the nineteenth century became the subject of a conflict between successive rectors seeking to restrict access and local people jealously guarding their perceived rights, but agreement was reached in 1894 and in 1965 the hills became a national nature reserve. Now continue steeply uphill through scrub, soon climbing steps, then bear half right up two more flights of steps to reach a gate. Do **not** use this, but turn left and follow a right-hand fence up further steps to a kissing-gate at the end of a ridge where you should turn round for a panoramic view with Sharpenhoe Clappers to your left, Barton-le-Clay and Pulloxhill ahead and Shillington with its prominent church to your right.

Now resume your previous direction following a left-hand fence straight on across downland, eventually passing through another kissing-gate and reaching a corner of the fence at the rim of a deep coombe formed 10,000 years ago by the melting of a glacier at the end of the last Ice Age. Here turn left and follow the fence to a kissing-gate. Do **not** go through this kissing-gate, but turn right beside the fence, passing the top of the coombe with the hill-fort called Ravensburgh Castle in woodland to your left. By a gate and kissing-gate, turn right, joining path BC19 and following a left-hand hedge above the coombe with fine views to your right and, at one point, across the hills ahead towards Streatley, Luton and the Dunstable Downs, eventually entering a belt of scrub through a kissing-gate. Now continue through the scrub, keeping left at a fork to reach a kissing-gate into a field. Here turn left onto path BC1, a grassy track along the edge of the scrub. On leaving the scrub behind, take bridleway BC16 straight on along the grassy track for half a mile, soon with views of Galley Hill and Warden Hill slightly to your right, eventually reaching a gate and motorcycle-trap leading to a road.

Leaving the Chiltern Way Extension, turn right onto this road for a quarter mile. At a left-hand bend by a clump of trees, turn left through a hedge gap onto bridleway SL40 along the edge of the clump. Now turn right through a hedge gap, then left to follow a left-hand hedge straight on through two fields with views ahead across Luton, to your right towards Streatley and later over your right shoulder towards Sharpenhoe Clappers. At the top of a rise in the second field, where Galley Hill and Warden Hill come into view ahead, follow the hedge bearing left and later right. On passing through a hedge gap by an electricity pylon, **joining the original Chiltern Way**, turn right onto bridleway SL32 along a grassy track beside a right-hand hedge for three-quarters of a mile, with views towards Galley Hill and Warden Hill and across Luton to your left, ignoring a branching track to your left and eventually passing Swedish Cottages to reach the A6 at a road junction. Cross this road carefully and take Sharpenhoe Road straight on into Streatley passing Streatleybury Farm. After a third of a mile, just past a left-hand pond, turn left into Bury Lane (path SL11), passing a pair of cottages, then continuing through gates. Where the lane opens out into a field, turn right through gates and follow a right-hand hedge uphill to a kissing-gate into an alleyway. Now cross the end of Churchill Close and where the alleyway turns left, take path SL12 through a wrought-iron gate into Streatley churchyard.

Streatley (pronounced ´Strettley` unlike its more famous Berkshire namesake and meaning ´clearing by the road`), once comprised just a few cottages and only in the last century did it start to grow into the medium-sized village we find today. It was for this reason that, in the early twentieth century, its fourteenth-century church with its earlier font, fifteenth-century tower and a mediæval wall painting of St. Catherine, was in ruins. It was only in 1938 that the church was restored by Sir Albert Richardson and it was here that Thomas Norton was buried in 1584.

Now bear right along a macadam path passing right of the church, then bearing left to gates leading out past the ´Chequers`. Here take the left-hand drive straight on to a road junction, then cross Sharpenhoe Road and take the left-hand footway of Church Road straight on. On leaving the village, follow the footway diverging from the road and passing left of an old road now used as a car park. By its far end, turn left through a hedge gap onto a fenced permissive bridleway, passing through the village allotments, then turning right, then immediately left to follow a right-hand hedge above the A6 cutting. On reaching the edge of a wood, turn left and follow it, then at a corner of the wood, go through a hedge gap and now on bridleway SL42, turn right, following a fenced track to the corner of the field, then turning sharp left and continuing along the fenced track. After a quarter mile, you then round the top of a steep wooded coombe called Watergutter Hole and cross the brow of Smithcombe Hill with splendid views opening out towards the Barton Hills ahead and the Bedfordshire lowlands to your left.

After a further quarter mile, ignore a gate and kissing-gate to your right and continue along the track bearing left with close-up views of the Barton Hills and across Barton-le-Clay village towards Shillington. Now ignore more gates to your right and bear left, eventually reaching a transverse hedge. Here take a permissive path straight on through a gap to a gate and kissing-gate, then turn right along a fenced track, looking out for a kissing-gate in the right-hand fence. Turn right through this, emerging onto open downland with more superb views. Here bear left along the top of the downland field, ignoring a waymarked fork to your left (where you leave the Icknield Way long-distance path) and continuing to the far end of the field. Here go through a kissing-gate, then bear right through a second, following a left-hand fence along the top of a steep coombe into scrubland to reach the edge of the mature beechwood known as Clappers Wood which crowns Sharpenhoe Clappers.

The name Sharpenhoe Clappers is of mixed origin, as the village name of Sharpenhoe is Saxon, meaning ´sharp spur of land`, while Clappers comes from Norman French meaning ´rabbit warren`. While the village at the foot of the hill, which unusually has always been a hamlet of the hilltop parish of Streatley, may therefore have originated in Saxon times, the hill shows much earlier signs of habitation, as it is capped by an Iron Age hill fort and both Iron Age and Roman pottery have been found there, but the Normans adapted it for breeding rabbits and thus arose the second part of its name. Clappers Wood within the earthworks, though ancient in appearance, was, in fact, only planted between 1834 and 1844 and a painting from 1815 shows it completely bare. In the wood is an obelisk erected by W.A. Robertson in memory of his two brothers who were killed in the First World War and this was also his reason for donating the Clappers to the National Trust in 1939. The former moated manor near Bury Farm just north of the village below was home to both the leading seventeenth-century mathematician, Edmund Wingate and Thomas Norton (1532 - 1584), the Calvinist zealot, who was both Solicitor General to Elizabeth I, nicknamed ´Rackmaster General` due to his ready use of torture against Roman Catholics, and a poet and playwright credited with being the forerunner of and model for Shakespeare and Marlowe.

Now bear slightly left up a steep bank where numerous tree roots act as steps, then bear slightly right along the inside edge of the wood. At the far end of the wood, follow the path bearing left, then, at a second corner where fine views open out ahead across Sharpenhoe towards Harlington and Toddington and the Chiltern Way forks, turn right onto path SL14, **rejoining the Chiltern Way Extension**, soon descending a long flight of steps through scrub to reach a field. Here follow a left-hand hedge straight on to reach Barton Road on the edge of Sharpenhoe.

Turn left onto this road, then, at a junction, turn right onto bridleway SL19, following the drive to Sharpenhoe Bury. At Bury Farm pass right of an electronic gate, then bear right across a concrete yard to the end of a brick wall and bear left, passing left of some large barns. Now take a rough track straight on towards Pulloxhill Water Tower, ignoring two branching tracks and a sleeper bridge to your left.

Having passed through a hedge gap, turn right onto path BC11, following a right-hand hedge at first, then bearing slightly right across the field with panoramic views towards the Barton Hills ahead, Sharpenhoe Clappers to your right and Pulloxhill to your left, to reach a gap by the tallest tree in the far hedge. Here cross a footbridge and go through a hedge gap, then turn right, following the right-hand hedge along the edge of a plantation. On reaching a powerline, turn left and follow it, soon walking between hedges and passing two World War II concrete 'pillboxes'. Eventually you emerge through a hedge gap, then, by a marker post, bear left into a green lane, immediately forking right through a kissing-gate. Now cross the next field diagonally to a gate and kissing-gate under the powerline, then follow a left-hand hedge beneath the powerline to a kissing-gate and footbridge into a spinney. Keep straight on through this, then, on entering a field, follow a right-hand hedge straight on still beneath the powerline. At the far end of the field, bear left to a kissing-gate into the car park of a weatherboarded watermill on the edge of Barton-le-Clay built in about 1790.

Now go straight on across the car park, an island of grass, a gravel track and another strip of grass and take path BC13 straight on along a gravel track, soon bearing right to a squeeze-stile leading to the A6. Here bear left to reach steps up to the road, then cross it via a staggered gap in the central-reservation crash-barrier. Now take macadam path BC33 straight on along an alleyway, soon joining a macadam drive. Having crossed an estate road, take path BC33 straight on between bollards to a road junction. Now keep straight on along Mill Lane to the B655 (Bedford Road), onto which you turn right. At a mini-roundabout by the 'Royal Oak', fork left into a side road, part of the ancient London road, then, at a T-junction, take Hexton Road (B655) straight on to reach your starting point.

WALK 7

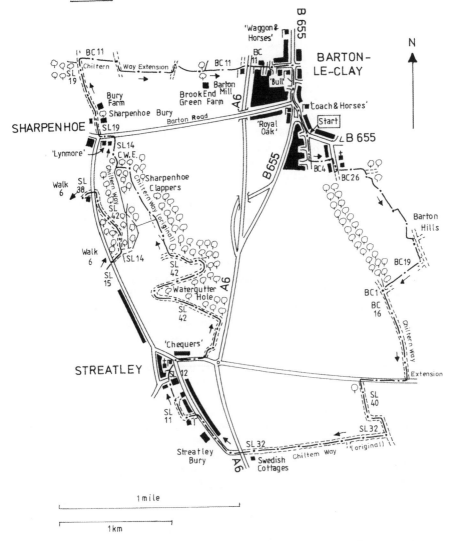

WALK 8   Stopsley

Length of Walk: 7.2 miles / 11.6 Km
Starting Point: Entrance to public car park by Barclays Bank,
                      Hitchin Road, Stopsley.
Grid Ref: TL104238
Maps: OS Landranger Sheet 166
            OS Explorer Sheet 193
            Chiltern Society FP Maps Nos. 25 & 30
How to get there / Parking: Stopsley, nearly 2 miles north of
Luton town centre, may be reached by leaving the M1 at
Junction 10 and taking the A1081 towards Luton, then the
A505 towards Hitchin. After a roundabout where the A6 is
signposted to your left and you turn right, ignore the first
turning for Stopsley, then at the next roundabout turn left
into Stopsley where there is a signposted car park to your
left after 90 yards.

Today, Stopsley, with its modern commercial and residential
development straddling the A505, has a very suburban appearance
hardly conducive to walking, but this appearance is deceptive, as,
after only 250 yards, you can leave the town behind and strike out
into open country. Indeed, till the early twentieth century, Stopsley
was a separate village on a hilltop above Luton and it was not till
1933 that Stopsley became incorporated into the Borough and,
even in 1951, Ordnance Survey maps show a small gap between
the village and the expanding industrial town. Despite its modern
appearance, Stopsley has a very long history as traces of Stone Age
habitation have been found and its name meaning ´glade on the
ridge` is of Saxon origin. From the seventeenth century onwards, the
high-quality straw which grew on its chalk uplands also became
valuable for use in the burgeoning straw hat industry in Luton and,
with the coming of the railway in 1858, this industry expanded still
further, while the heavy clay capping its hilltop made Stopsley a
centre for brickmaking where the local ´Luton Greys` were
produced. Despite the twentieth-century decline of the hat industry
and closure of the brickworks, the industrial expansion of Luton has
ensured that Stopsley has remained prosperous, while the high
scenic value of its common and Warden and Galley Hill to the
north have so far ensured the preservation of a ´green lung` between

the pincer-like urban expansion along the A6 and A505.
The walk explores the scenic hill country on the Bedfordshire/
Hertfordshire border, leading you from Stopsley across Stopsley
Common with its fine views, before dropping to skirt the edge of
Luton and climbing to join the original Chiltern Way on a ridge
near Warden Hill. You then follow a loop of the Way via
Butterfield Green, Lilley and the southern end of the Lilley Hoo
ridge to the edge of Putteridge Bury Park with numerous fine views
throughout, before leaving the Way and continuing through the
park back to Stopsley.

Starting from the entrance to the public car park by Barclays Bank in
Stopsley, cross Hitchin Road, then turn right and take the next turning
left (Venetia Road). At a T-junction, turn right into Lothair Road,
then, just past house no.37a, turn left into an unsignposted alleyway
leading to Stopsley Common. Now take path LU23, following the
left-hand side of a hedge straight on across the common. By the far
end of the hedge, turn left across the open common to reach the
corner of a fence with a gate and kissing-gate, with wide views across
Luton opening out ahead. Do **not** go through these gates, but keep
right of the fence and follow it straight on downhill. By a second
kissing-gate, fork right through a kissing-gate into scrubland and
continue downhill, ignoring a crossing path with a kissing-gate to
your left, then descending more steeply with several flights of steps to
reach an open field. Now bear slightly right across the field to reach
the corner of a wall on the edge of a housing estate. Here bear half
left and follow the edge of the estate to reach Bushmead Road on the
edge of Luton.
    Turn right onto this road, then, after 20 yards, turn right again
between bollards onto path LU22, following a green lane at first, then
continuing along a gravel path. By redundant stile steps now used as a
seat, follow the right-hand hedge straight on through scrub to a hedge
gap into an open field. Here take bridleway SL30 straight on along a
worn grassy track with fine views towards Warden Hill ahead and to
your left across Luton towards Blows Down and the Dunstable Downs,
soon joining bridleway SL29. At the far side of the field at a track
junction, take a grassy track straight on beside a right-hand hedge for
over half a mile with wide views over your left shoulder across Luton
towards Blows Down and the Dunstable Downs, eventually climbing
to reach a crossways at the top of the ridge where Galley Hill comes
into view ahead.
    Here, **joining the original Chiltern Way**, turn right onto bridleway
SL31, taking a farm road straight on for half a mile past Whitehill
Wood to your left to reach the end of Butterfield Green Road by the

entrance to Whitehill Farm. Take this road straight on. After 50 yards by a telephone pole, turn left through a concealed kissing-gate onto path LU26, bearing half left across a field and soon becoming path SL34. In the far corner of the field, go through a fence gap and bear slightly left across the next field, passing just right of an oak tree to reach a gap in the bottom hedge, with fine views ahead in mid-field across Lilley Bottom and Lilley towards Great Offley on the next ridge. Go straight on through a gap in the bottom hedge and, now in Hertfordshire, take path LL3, following a left-hand hedge, then the edge of Lilley Park Wood straight on. At the far end of the wood, now on path LL2, continue along a green lane, eventually emerging into the car park of Lilley Village Hall. Go straight on through this car park to reach the village street, then turn left onto its footway.

Lilley, situated just off the A505 (Luton - Hitchin main road), is clearly recognisable as an old estate village with a large number of its cottages bearing the rampant silver lion crest of the Docwra (pronounced 'Dockray') and later the Sowerby families, both of Cumbrian origin, who, at various times, owned nearby Putteridge Bury. The former twelfth-century church was almost entirely rebuilt by Thomas Jekyll in 1870, but retains the Norman chancel arch and fifteenth-century font of the original building. In the seventeenth century, Lilley was a centre of non-conformity, being home to the religious writer, James Janeway, and it is believed that John Bunyan, author of 'Pilgrim's Progress', secretly preached in the cellar of one of the village cottages. An infamous later resident of the village was the nineteenth-century alchemist, Johann Kellermann, who disappeared from Lilley as suddenly as he came.

After 60 yards, opposite the near corner of Lilley churchyard, turn right onto fenced path LL4, soon reaching a kissing-gate into a field. Here go straight on, following a left-hand fence at first, then continuing across the field to a kissing-gate left of an oak tree. Now bear half right across the next field to a kissing-gate in the far corner. Here bear left, keeping right of a hedge and following it over the Lilley Hoo ridge, at the top of which was once open downland with an eighteenth-century racecourse where the Prince Regent (later King George IV) raced his horses. At the top of the ridge, fine views open out towards Great Offley ahead and down Lilley Bottom to your right. Now follow the hedge downhill to reach Lilley Hoo Lane near Lilley Hoo Farm. Turn right onto this cul-de-sac road and follow it for a quarter mile, passing through a tunnel under the A505 to reach a T-junction with the old main road at the foot of Hollybush Hill. Here turn left, then, after 100 yards, turn right into Glebe Farm, immediately forking right onto byway OF51, a gravel lane right of the buildings. Now continue for over half a mile to a road called

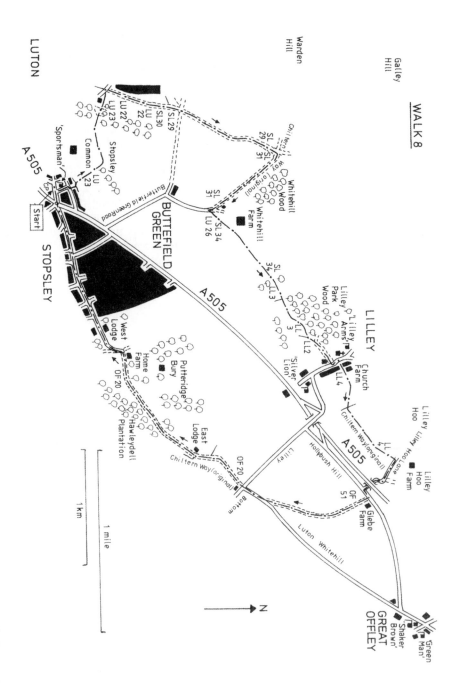

WALK 8

LUTON

Galley Hill

Warden Hill

Butterfield Green Road

A505

'Sportsman'

Start

STOPSLEY

LU 22

LU 22

LU 23

SL30

SL29

SL SL 29 31

Chiltern Way (original)

Whitehill Wood

SL 31

Common

LU 23

Stopsley

BUTTEFIELD GREEN

SL34

LU 26

Whitehill Farm

A505

West Lodge

Home Farm

Putteridge Bury

East Lodge

OF 20

Hawleydell Plantation

Chiltern Way (original)

OF 20

Bottom

SL 34 LL3

Lilley Park Wood

LL2

'Lilley Arms'

LL 3

LILLEY

'Silver Lion'

Church Farm

LL4

Chiltern Way (original)

Lilley

Hollybush Hill

A505

LL

Lilley Hoo

Lilley Hoo Lane

OF 51

Glebe Farm

Lilley Hoo Farm

Luton Whitehill

GREAT OFFLEY

'Shaker Brown'

'Green Man'

N

1 km

1 mile

53

Luton White Hill, part of an ancient route from Luton via Putteridge Bury to Great Offley and Hitchin. Turn right onto this, then, at a crossways in Lilley Bottom, take byway OF20 straight on for a third of a mile.

On reaching the park wall of Putteridge Bury at East Lodge, **leaving the Chiltern Way**, take the rough road (still byway OF20) straight on for two-thirds of a mile, passing East Lodge and soon going through and then along the edge of Hawleydell Plantation, before climbing with brief glimpses of Putteridge Bury house (rebuilt in the Elizabethan style in 1908-11 and now part of Luton University) through the trees to your right, to reach the end of a macadam road by Home Farm. Here continue along this road, bearing left by a white house, then keeping right at a fork, soon passing houses at West Lodge, then through a gap in an overgrown section of the park wall marking the Luton boundary. Now take Putteridge Road straight on for three-quarters of a mile to the roundabout at Stopsley. Here turn right to cross the A505, then turn left along Hitchin Road to reach your starting point.

WALK 9   Breachwood Green

Length of Walk: 7.6 miles / 12.3 Km
Starting Point: ´Red Lion`, Breachwood Green.
Grid Ref: TL151220
Maps: OS Landranger Sheet 166
OS Explorer Sheet 193
Chiltern Society FP Map No.30
How to get there / Parking: Breachwood Green, 3.5 miles east
of the centre of Luton, may be reached by leaving the M1 at
Junction 10 and taking the A1081 towards Luton, then the
A505 towards Hitchin to Eaton Green Road Roundabout,
then turning right into Eaton Green Road signposted to Tea
Green. At the next roundabout, bear left, then, at a further
roundabout, turn right. Now go straight on, soon leaving
Luton behind. At a fork, keep right and follow the priority
road for 1.5 miles to Breachwood Green. In the centre of the
village by the ´Red Lion`, turn left into Oxford Road and
find a suitable place to park.
Notes: Heavy nettle growth may be encountered on paths KW19
and KW38 in the summer months.

Breachwood Green, a hamlet of King's Walden parish on a
ridgetop above Lilley Bottom, would seem a very remote location
when approached through the maze of lanes between Luton and
Stevenage and indeed the history and appearance of the surrounding countryside would tend to confirm this, but it will not be long
before you realise that the village lies beneath the flightpath of the
approach to Luton Airport. Despite this, however, Breachwood
Green, whose name derives from the Ancient British chief Breah
and whose Edwardian baptist church can boast a pulpit used by the
non-conformist preacher and author, John Bunyan at nearby
Bendish in 1658, makes a good centre for exploring the rolling hills
around Lilley Bottom, which is reminiscent of Hampden Bottom in
the Chiltern heartlands but far less well-known.

    This walk, which is generally easy in nature and includes a
typical Chiltern mix of woods and fields, leads you from
Breachwood Green across Lilley Bottom to the mother village of
King's Walden with its church and manor house, before circling
through remote country to join the original Chiltern Way at

Cockernhoe and follow it back to your starting point.

Starting from the ´Red Lion` in Breachwood Green, take the King's Walden road. Just past Colemans Road to your left, turn right over a stile by a gate onto enclosed path KW15, then, just past a pond to your left, turn left over a stile, passing the pond, crossing a second stile, negotiating climb-through rails and continuing across a field to two stiles and a kissing-gate by a large hawthorn bush. Now turn right beside a right-hand hedge. After 80 yards by another marker post, turn left across the field, heading for a marker post at a bend in the top fence. Here turn right onto path KW14, following the fence to a gate into Lord's Wood, then take a waymarked path straight on through the wood. At the far side of the wood, ignoring a branching path to your right, leave the wood and follow its outside edge, then a left-hand hedge, straight on downhill to reach a road in Lilley Bottom. Now cross a stile opposite and keep straight on uphill, heading just right of the top corner of the field to reach a gap in the trees leading to a wooden signpost. Here turn left onto path KW19, following a right-hand fence through woodland, soon with fences on both sides. On passing through a gate into a parkland field, bear right and follow a right-hand fence. Now, by an oak tree, bear slightly left across the field, noticing a haha to the right of King's Walden Bury, which is hidden in the trees, eventually reaching a gate leading to a bend in King's Walden's village street.

The name King's Walden is derived from the village having been a royal manor in a wooded area. Its thirteenth-century church, with its notable fourteenth-century painted screen and a tower from the same period, contains memorials to the Hale family who lived at the Bury from 1595 to 1885. The house bearing this name today, however, is not that of the Hales as their Elizabethan house was demolished and rebuilt in 1889, only for the same thing to happen again in 1972 when the present neo-Georgian house was built.

Now go straight on uphill, passing the church to your right. After 200 yards, turn left through a hedge gap onto path KW24, entering a field and bearing left beside a sporadic left-hand hedge with fine views to your left across Lilley Bottom towards Breachwood Green and Darleyhall Windmill to reach the left-hand corner of Tache Wood. Here turn right onto path KW22 along the edge of the wood to a bend in a farm road. Turn left onto this, passing through the wood and continuing with more fine views to your left across Lilley Bottom towards Breachwood Green and Darleyhall Windmill. By a Dutch barn, take a grassy track straight on, passing through a hedge gap right of an oak tree. Where the hedge bears right, follow it towards Lane House to a road near a junction at Ley Green. Here bear half right onto the Hitchin and Preston road. Just past some cottages to your right, turn left through gates onto path KW25, following a fenced path bearing right to a kissing-gate. Now take the fenced path straight on across a field to a kissing-gate under an oak tree, then continue ahead through a further kissing-gate to a fourth in the far right-hand corner of the field right of a wooden building. Here go straight on, keeping left of a hedge. At the far end of the field, bear slightly right through a hedge gap, then, by a collapsed stile, turn right into a green lane, bearing left to reach a road at Kingswell End.

Turn left onto this road, then, after 100 yards, turn right onto a concrete drive (still path KW25), soon climbing steps, passing right of a cottage and continuing across a field to a hedge gap under an oak tree, then bear slightly left across the next field to a hedge gap by an electricity pole leading to a road. Turn right onto this and follow it for a quarter mile. Near the end of a long right-hand bend, turn left through a gap by collapsed wooden rails onto path KW38, following a sunken lane into a field. Now take a grassy track straight on to the left-hand corner of Judkin's Wood. Here enter a green lane and follow it straight on along the wood edge. On reemerging into the field, continue along the outside edge of the wood to a corner, then bear half left across the corner of the field to a hedge gap. Now take a grassy track straight on with panoramic views opening out up, down and across Lilley Bottom. On reaching the right-hand corner of Furzen Wood, follow the track, bearing left along its edge and soon becoming enclosed by a left-hand hedge. Ignore a crossing track, then, 100 yards farther on, fork right onto a track into the wood. On reemerging into a field with a bungalow ahead, bear right and follow the outside edge of the wood downhill to the road in Lilley Bottom.

Turn right onto this road and follow it for 400 yards, then turn left through a gap by gates onto path OF7, following the left side of a hedge gently uphill into a wood. Now follow a sunken way within the wood edge, climbing and bearing right then left with fine views in places to your right towards a large modern house called Offley Chase and Lilley beyond. On leaving the wood, follow the right-hand hedge straight on to enter another wood and continue along its edge. Where the hedge bears away to the right, follow it, soon entering a short green lane leading to a road called Chalk Hill. Turn right onto this road, then, after 180 yards, just past a holly tree to your left, turn left onto path OF27 up steps and across a field to the left-hand corner of Messina Plantation. Here continue along its outside edge, then, at the far side of the wood, follow a right-hand hedge straight on through two fields. At the far end of the second field, go through a kissing-gate and turn left onto path OF25, following a left-hand hedge to another kissing-gate, then continue between hedges to a road at the end of Cockernhoe Green.

Cockernhoe with its green and scattered cottages gives a deceptively rural impression, which belies the fact that it is now a mere quarter mile from the edge of Luton with its voracious appetite for building land. It is largely the existence of the county boundary which it has to thank for so far being spared the fate of nearby Stopsley, which has long been swamped by urban development.

Cross this road and turn right along the back edge of the green, eventually crossing two gravel drives and **joining** the Luton road and **the original Chiltern Way**. Just past the last house in the village, where the edge of Luton can be seen a field's length ahead, turn left through a gate onto path OF2, immediately forking left off the grassy track onto a fenced path through scrub, then a strip of woodland. On emerging onto a crossing grassy track between woods, turn right into a field and then left, following the edge of Brickkiln Wood with views to your right towards Luton and Luton Airport, soon forking left onto a fenced path through the wood. By the corner of a left-hand field, bear right, soon emerging into the corner of a right-hand field. Here turn left, then, after 15 yards, bear left again onto a fenced path into a tree belt, soon bearing right and later bearing right again to enter a field. Now turn left and follow a left-hand hedge with more views of Luton and its airport. At the far end of the field, take a drive straight on past some cottages to a road junction by Wandon End Farm.

Here bear half right across a traffic island and the priority road to enter a field. Now turn left onto path KW41, following the edge of the field parallel to the road for 200 yards. By a slight left-hand bend in the road, bear slightly right across the field, passing Wandon End to your left to rejoin the field edge by an oak tree and follow it to rejoin the road at a road junction. Here take the Breachwood Green road straight on. At a left-hand bend, leave the road and take bridleway KW52, following a winding grassy track straight on for 300 yards to reach the corner of a hedge. Now go through a hedge gap and follow a sporadic left-hand hedge uphill. At the next hedgeline, leave the bridleway and take path KW6, bearing slightly right across a field, heading just left of a pair of oak trees and joining the top of a grass bank left of the oak trees. Now follow this bank for 200 yards to reach a fence. Here turn right and follow this fence, soon turning left. Where it turns left again, continue along a grass path past a large oak tree. Some 30 yards beyond this tree, bear half left across the field to a kissing-gate onto Chapel Road on the edge of Breachwood Green, where, **leaving the Chiltern Way**, you turn left for your starting point.

WALK 9

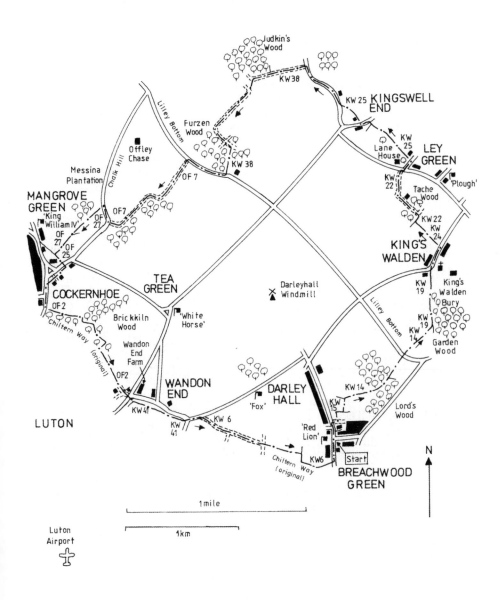

LILLEY

Judkin's Wood

KW 38

KW 25 KINGSWELL END

Furzen Wood

Offley Chase

KW 25 LEY GREEN

Lane House

Messina Plantation

OF 7

KW 38

KW 22

'Plough'

Tache Wood

MANGROVE GREEN

'King William IV'

OF 27

OF 7

OF 27

KW 22

KW 24

OF 27

KING'S WALDEN

OF 25

TEA GREEN

Darleyhall Windmill

KW 19

King's Walden Bury

COCKERNHOE

OF 2

Brickkiln Wood

'White Horse'

KW 19

KW 14

Chiltern Way (original)

Wandon End Farm

Garden Wood

OF2

WANDON END

KW 14

KW 15

Lord's Wood

'Fox'

DARLEY HALL

LUTON

KW 41

KW 6

'Red Lion'

KW 41

Start

N

KW6

Chiltern Way (original)

BREACHWOOD GREEN

1 mile

1km

Luton Airport

59

WALK 10   Pegsdon

Length of Walk: 5.7 miles / 9.2 Km
Starting Point: Entrance to cul-de-sac road at Pegsdon village green.
Grid Ref: TL119303
Maps: OS Landranger Sheet 166
OS Explorer Sheet 193
Chiltern Society FP Map No.26
How to get there / Parking: Pegsdon, 4 miles west of Hitchin, may be reached from the town by taking the B655 towards Barton-le-Clay for 4 miles, then turning right into a road signposted to Pegsdon and Shillington. After 100 yards, turn left into a wide cul-de-sac road where you can park.

Pegsdon, a tiny village with a green and a pub at the foot of the Chiltern escarpment below Deacon Hill, has always been a hamlet of the Bedfordshire parish of Shillington surrounded on three sides by Hertfordshire. To the east of the village is a hill called Knocking Hoe capped by a Neolithic long barrow known as Knocking Knoll. Legend has it that the ghostly knocking sounds said to emanate from inside giving it its name are made by an Ancient British chieftain guarding a great chest of treasure against tomb raiders. On the sides of steep-sided coombes between Knocking Hoe and Deacon Hill to the south, are mediæval ´strip lynchets` (terraces cut into the hillside to enable steeply-sloping ground to be ploughed), giving evidence of early cultivation of what would appear to be a rather infertile terrain.

This walk takes advantage of a scenic loop at the northeastern extremity of the Chiltern Way Extension to form a circular walk almost entirely following the Way. From Pegsdon at the foot of a spectacular open section of the escarpment, the walk follows the Way over Knocking Hoe with its ancient barrow and High Down, both with superb views, before heading southwestwards to Little Offley with its Tudor manor house. A short link then takes you across Lilley Hoo to rejoin the Way at Telegraph Hill, from which you descend with more fine views to your starting point.

Starting from the entrance to the cul-de-sac road on Pegsdon village green, **take the Chiltern Way Extension**, turning left onto the Shillington road. At a left-hand bend, turn right into Pegsdon Way and follow it through the village, passing the ´Live and Let Live`. Now, at a right-hand bend near its junction with the B655, turn left onto path SH16, following a private road towards Pegsdon Common Farm for over a quarter mile, bearing right then left with fine views of Deacon Hill to your right. On rounding a left-hand bend, by a signpost, turn right onto a grass crop-break across a field to reach a flight of steps, now additionally with fine views towards Knocking Hoe to your left. Climb the steps, then ignore a crossing track and climb a second flight. Now continue uphill with a plantation to your left and a fenced coombe to your right. After leaving the plantation behind, follow the top edge of the coombe straight on for 150 yards until you reach the second marker post, then turn left and follow the left-hand side of a sporadic hedge with superb panoramic views towards Knocking Hoe and a water tower near Stondon ahead, Pulloxhill with its prominent water tower, Higham Gobion and Shillington to your left and Deacon Hill behind you. At the far end of the field, turn right onto a sunken track, climbing gently with a deep coombe with strip lynchets and a close-up view of Knocking Hoe to your left, to reach a gate and gap with a low rail at the top of the hill by the corner of Tingley Field Plantation, (a Viking name meaning ´meeting-place in a clearing`) where it is worth turning round for a superb view towards Sharpenhoe Clappers, Pulloxhill, Shillington and beyond.

Now go through the gap and turn left onto bridleway SH2, which is enclosed by a right-hand fence at first, but is later open to your right. At the far side of the right-hand field, crossing into Hertfordshire, turn left onto bridleway PI8, following a wide green lane known as Wood Lane gently downhill for nearly half a mile, with a brief view at one point through a gap in the right-hand hedge towards Letchworth. Now, just after a left-hand bend and a seat, turn right through a hedge gap between beech trees onto path PI9, following a grassy track beside a left-hand hedge downhill and up again, with views through gaps in the hedge towards Pirton and Letchworth. On reaching a corner of Tingley Wood, take the grassy track straight on along its outside edge, with High Down House coming into view to your left and views over your left shoulder towards Pirton, the water tower near Stondon, Holwell and Letchworth.

High Down House, unusually for this part of the country, a stone house with twisted chimney stacks and mullioned windows, was built in 1612 by Thomas Docwra (pronounced ´Dockray`), a descendant of

Sir Thomas Docwra, Lord Grand Prior in England of the Knights of St. John in Jerusalem, in an imposing position previously occupied by an earlier house. In 1648 the house is said to have been the scene of the murder of a cavalier named Goring, who had been hiding here from Parliamentarian troops, and his headless ghost is said to ride to Hitchin Priory on a white horse once a year.

On entering a second field, by a large oak tree, ignore a branching track to your left, but leave the edge of the wood and go straight on across the field to a kissing-gate left of a dead tree in the far hedge at the top of High Down. Here take path PI7 straight on through the kissing-gate, then follow the left-hand side of a hedge downhill and up again to a gap in a belt of trees concealing a section of the B655 which follows the ancient Icknield Way. In this gap, fork left onto a permissive path between fences at first within the tree belt to emerge onto the B655 opposite your continuation.

Cross this road and take path OF37 straight on through a hedge gap opposite, then bear slightly right across the field to pass the right-hand side of a clump of trees on the skyline concealing an old pond. Now bear slightly left to reach a marker post by a large elm stump where there are fine views to your left towards Hitchin. Here disregard a crossing path and bear slightly right to reach a kissing-gate in the far corner of the field. Ignoring a crossing track, go through the kissing-gate. Now follow a green lane bearing left then right, then continue to Park View Stables. Here keep straight on, by the house following a left-hand wall to a kissing-gate into a belt of trees, through which you continue to a macadam private road (bridleway OF34). Turn left onto this road, immediately forking right onto a rough road. Now follow this road for a quarter mile, ignoring branching drives to your left leading to Wellbury House and passing through trees. Where another field opens out to your right and the road is once again macadamed, follow it straight on. Just past a speed hump, turn right onto bridleway OF36, crossing the field to the bottom corner of a copse called Saddle Plantation. Here bear slightly left, following its outside edge. At its far end, keep straight on uphill to pass right of the end of a hedge and join a grassy farm track leading straight on towards Little Offley.

At the next transverse hedge, **leaving the Chiltern Way Extension**, go straight on into the farmyard of Little Offley Farm, where you bear right then left to pass between a black stable block and a black barn. On leaving the farm behind, follow the farm track straight on, passing the back of Little Offley House, a fine late Tudor brick manor house set in parkland, then bearing right. On reaching a wide waymarked gap in the left-hand hedge, turn left through it and take a gravel track following a left-hand hedge. On entering woodland, take

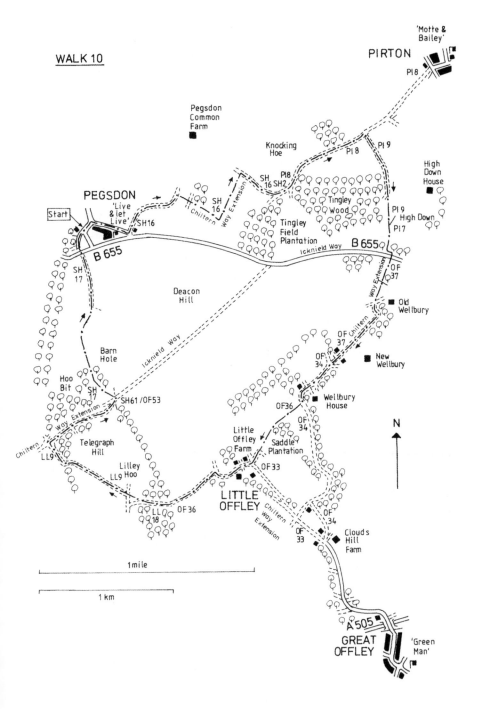

WALK 10

'Motte & Bailey'

PIRTON

PI8

Pegsdon
Common
Farm

Knocking
Hoe

PI8

PI9

High
Down
House

SH
16 SH2

PI8

PEGSDON

'Live
& let
Live'

SH16

SH
16

Chiltern

Way Extension

Tingley
Wood

PI9
High Down

PI7

Tingley
Field
Plantation

Start

B 655

Icknield Way

B 655

OF
37

SH
17

Way Extension

Deacon
Hill

Old
Wellbury

Icknield Way

OF
37

Chiltern

Barn
Hole

OF
34

New
Wellbury

Hoo
Bit

SH
17

OF36

Wellbury
House

SH61/OF53

Way Extension

OF
34

Chiltern

Telegraph
Hill

Little
Offley
Farm

Saddle
Plantation

N

LL9

Lilley
LL9 Hoo

OF33

LITTLE
OFFLEY

LL
18

OF36

OF
34

Chiltern
Way
Extension

OF
33

Clouds
Hill
Farm

1 mile

1 km

A 505

GREAT
OFFLEY

'Green
Man'

63

bridleway LL18 straight on through it to reach a large upland field called Lilley Hoo, where horse-racing took place in the eighteenth century and the Prince Regent (later King George IV) raced his horses. Here bear half right across the field to the corner of a hedge by a spreading oak tree, where you join bridleway LL9 and take a grassy track straight on. Eventually you pass the corner of woodland to your left and enter a sunken way, gradually bearing left with views to your left towards Warden Hill, Galley Hill and Streatley, then bearing right into woodland and descending. On reaching a T-junction in a clearing, **rejoining the Chiltern Way Extension**, turn right onto a grassy permissive track up Telegraph Hill to its top where there are fine views behind you towards Warden and Galley Hills.

Telegraph Hill, at 184 metres (602 feet) the highest point in North Hertfordshire District, is so named as it was used during the Napoleonic Wars as a semaphore and heliograph signalling station. Previously known as Pegsdon Beacon, it is thought to have been used in 1588 for one of a chain of beacons warning of the approach of the Spanish Armada and again in the Civil War in 1643 to warn of Prince Rupert's advance on Dunstable.

Now ignore a branching track to your right and keep straight on, soon following the edge of Lilley Hoo. At the far side of this field, bear left through a hedge gap to join the Icknield Way (byway SH61/OF53 straddling the Bedfordshire boundary). Turn right onto this, then, after 50 yards, reentering Bedfordshire, turn left through a kissing-gate onto path SH17, crossing a field to a corner of a fence. Now follow this fence straight on, ignoring a kissing-gate in it, eventually with views to your right towards Pegsdon, Shillington and the water tower near Stondon. On passing through a kissing-gate, keep straight on above a deep coombe known as Barn Hole, soon with superb panoramic views across lowland Bedfordshire, gradually descending and passing through another kissing-gate. Now once again follow a right-hand fence. On passing through further gates, take a grassy track straight on downhill towards distant Gravenhurst, eventually reaching a kissing-gate onto the B655 at Pegsdon. Now cross this road and a strip of verge opposite, then continue along a cul-de-sac road to your starting point.

WALK 11   Hitchin

Length of Walk: 6.9 miles / 11.2 Km
Starting Point: End of cul-de-sac section of Gosmore Road,
Hitchin, south of Hitchin Hill Roundabout.
Grid Ref: TL185283
Maps: OS Landranger Sheet 166
OS Explorer Sheet 193
Chiltern Society FP Map Nos. 26, 29 & 30
How to get there / Parking: From the Hitchin Hill Roundabout
at the junction of the A602 and B656, take the road
signposted to Gosmore, then take the first turning right, a
cul-de-sac section of Gosmore Road where you can park.

Hitchin, on the River Hiz, a tributary of the Ivel and Great Ouse, at
the north-eastern extremity of the Chilterns, is probably the most
beautiful town in the Chilterns. Already settled in the Bronze Age,
Hitchin and its river only derived their names in the Anglo-Saxon
period when the town became home to the Hicce tribe. It was,
however, in the Middle Ages that Hitchin became rich as a centre of
the wool trade which supplied the Flanders weavers. This can be
seen in St. Mary's Church, a thirteenth-century building lavishly
remodelled by rich wool merchants in the fifteenth century.
Amongst its many treasures, this massive church contains numerous
brasses and a fifteenth-century font with a beautiful carved spire-
shaped canopy. Apart from its church, Hitchin, the centre of which
retains its mediæval street pattern, can boast a wealth of picturesque
buildings including half-timbered houses with overhangs dating
back to the fifteenth and sixteenth centuries and so is well worth
exploring before or after your walk.

The walk soon leaves the town behind and leads you southwestwards past the hamlets of Charlton, birthplace in 1813 of Sir
Henry Bessemer, inventor of an improved steel-making process,
and Wellhead at the source of the River Hiz, to join the Chiltern
Way Extension near Temple End. You then follow it to a beautiful
coombe called Offley Holes before climbing the Chiltern escarp-
ment to Austage End and continuing across an upland plateau to
Preston with its picturesque green. Leaving the Chiltern Way
Extension, you then head north, passing through a wood where
Bunyan held secret services, before descending along an ancient

lane to pass a hunting lodge of Henry VIII and return to Hitchin.

Starting from the end of the cul-de-sac section of Gosmore Road at Hitchin Hill, take the continuing tarmac path. Just before reaching a footbridge over the A602, by a signpost, turn left onto path H120, the right-hand of two branching paths, following the A602 fence through a tree belt then a large parkland field in Priory Park where fine views open out ahead towards Birkitt Hill and Telegraph Hill. At the bottom of a dip by a marker post, bear half left onto path H39, heading for an apparent junction of fences where you bear half right along a fenced grassy track, gradually bearing left, passing through a tree belt, crossing a culvert over the River Hiz and eventually reaching a kissing-gate by field gates onto Charlton Road.

Cross this and go through gates opposite onto a farm drive, immediately turning left onto path H32, heading for the right-hand side of a clump of trees to reach a kissing-gate by a wooden shed. Now keep straight on, following a garden fence at first, then continuing across a field to a corner just right of a cluster of cottages at Charlton where you go through a kissing-gate. Here do **not** join the road, but turn right onto bridleway H33, following a stony lane gently uphill. By a cottage the lane becomes macadamed, but, where this macadamed route turns right, leave it and go straight on through a gap by a gate. Now follow a green lane straight on for a third of a mile, then, on emerging into a field, continue beside a right-hand hedge. Where this hedge turns right, leave it and keep straight on to a gap in the next hedge.

Here, **joining the Chiltern Way Extension**, turn left into Hoar's Lane (byway H28) and follow it downhill for a quarter mile to the crossways with an unmade road called Chalk Hill near Temple End. Here take the continuation of Hoar's Lane, also an unmade public road, straight on through a hedge gap and beside a right-hand hedge, soon entering a green lane. Where its left-hand hedge ends, take a grassy track straight on, soon entering another section of green lane, then passing a copse to reach a bend in a narrow road.

Here turn right onto bridleway PR6, following a grassy track through a gate into a field where views of Offleyholes Farm soon open out to your left. Where the track bears left through a gate, leave it and follow the left-hand fence straight on to a bridlegate into Pinnaclehill Plantation. Keep straight on through this copse to a gate into another field, then follow the left-hand fence straight on, ignoring a gate in it and reaching a bridlegate into West Wood. Go straight on through the corner of this wood, climbing steeply into a field. Now take a grassy track along the outside edge of the wood for 350 yards. Having passed a track into the wood, by a marker post where the track bears right, leave it and bear slightly left across the field to the right-hand of two gaps in the far hedge. Now take fenced bridleway KW28 straight on to a bend in a green lane (restricted byway KW47), which you follow straight on to the end of the road in the tiny hamlet of Austage End.

Some 25 yards along this road, turn left onto path KW37 between hedges. On emerging into a field, follow a left-hand hedge, later the edge of a plantation, straight on to a large oak tree. Now bear slightly right across the field to a hedge gap with a marker post midway between trees flanking a green lane (byway KW46). Turn left into this lane, then, after 100 yards at the far end of a long gap in the right-hand hedge by a marker post and a hollybush, turn right up steps onto the continuation of path KW37, crossing a field to a gap in the trees on the skyline left of a group of larger trees, where you reach a track junction. Here ignore the first right-hand track, pass between bollards and take the second (byway KW48), entering a wide green lane called Dead Woman's Lane. After 300 yards, just past a left-hand bend and a large oak tree to your right, turn left through a concealed kissing-gate onto path PR5, following a left-hand hedge to a gate and stile. Now keep straight on to the right-hand side of a gap between farm buildings, then bear half right across a field to a gap in the far hedge left of a sycamore tree to reach a concealed kissing-gate into Butcher's Lane, Preston (described in Walk 12). Turn left onto this narrow road, then, just before a left-hand bend by the end of the right-hand houses, turn right onto enclosed path PR4 leading to Church Meadow, a small millennium green. Follow its left-hand edge straight on to enter another enclosed path between hedges leading to Chequers Lane.

Leaving the Chiltern Way Extension, turn left onto this road and follow it round a left-hand bend. Where the right-hand houses end, turn right through a hedge gap onto path PR13 and follow a line of trees. At its far end turn left and follow a holly hedge, then, where it turns right, go straight on across the field to a kissing-gate in the far corner of the field by a corner of Wain Wood, in which the seventeenth-century preacher and writer of 'Pilgrim's Progress`, John Bunyan, regularly held secret midnight Puritan services with massive congregations. Now keep straight on across the next field, passing one outcrop of the wood to reach a kissing-gate at the second. Here bear slightly right and follow the outside edge of Wain Wood to enter an outcrop of the wood, then take an obvious path straight on through the wood, soon briefly with a fence and field to your left, before diverging from them. At the far end of the wood (now on path IP6), go straight on passing two kissing-gate frames, then continue uphill through a copse. On emerging into a field, follow the right-hand hedge straight on, then, at its far end, go straight on through a hedge gap into Tatmorehills Lane. Here turn right, joining bridleway IP5 and following it along the inside edge of a wood, then continue downhill along a green lane, later with views to your left towards Birkitt Hill, Deacon Hill and Pirton and ahead towards the outskirts of Hitchin. Where the right-hand hedge ends and views open out to your right towards Gosmore and St. Ippolyts with its prominent church, take path IP3, bearing half right across the field to a wide gap at a kink in the bottom hedge, joining a right-hand hedge and following it through the hedge gap and a second field to a hedge gap leading to Maydencroft Lane.

Turn right onto this road and follow it for 250 yards passing the half-timbered Maydencroft Manor to your left, which is reputed to have been used by Henry VIII as a hunting lodge. Where the road narrows, turn left up steps and through a kissing-gate onto path IP2, then follow a left-hand hedge straight on for some 200 yards to a green gate. Go through a kissing-gate beside it and bear right, passing just right of an area of scrub concealing an old pond, then bear half left to go through a kissing-gate by two gates in the next hedge. Now follow a fenced path round two sides of a field to reach Brick Kiln Lane, then take path H45 straight on between gardens to a residential road on the edge of Hitchin.

Here bear half left across a small green, a road and another small green and take the continuation of path H45 straight on between the gardens of nos. 27 and 29 to reach the edge of an old parkland field at Priory Park. Now take path H44, bearing half right across the field, with fine views to your left towards Great Offley and Deacon Hill, passing right of a midfield beech tree to reach a hedge gap leading into a tree belt. In the trees, turn left onto path H43 and follow it through the tree belt until you emerge by a signpost at the end of the A602 footbridge. Here turn sharp right through a fence gap onto a macadam path leading back to your starting point.

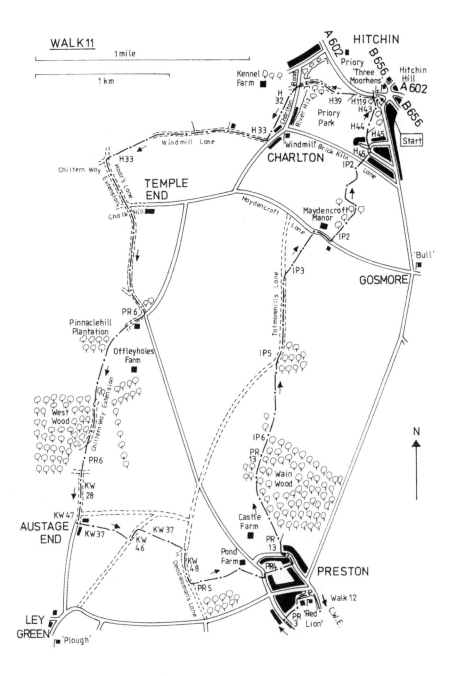

WALK 11

1 mile

1 km

HITCHIN
A 602
B 656
Priory 'Three Moorhens'
Hitchin Hill
A 602
B 656
Kennel Farm
H 32
Coalton Road
H 33
River H12
Windmill Lane
H 39
H119
H 43
Priory Park
H 44
H 45
Start
Windmill Brick Kiln
H 45
IP2
Lane
CHARLTON
H 33
Chiltern Way
Hoar's Lane
Chiltern Way Extension
TEMPLE END
Chalk Hill
Maydencroft Lane
Maydencroft Manor
IP2
'Bull'
IP3
GOSMORE
Tatmorehills Lane
PR 6
Pinnaclehill Plantation
Offleyholes Farm
IP5
West Wood
Chiltern Way Extension
IP6
PR 13
Wain Wood
N
PR 6
KW 28
KW 47
AUSTAGE END
KW37
KW 46
KW 37
KW 48
Castle Farm
PR 13
Pond Farm
PR
PRESTON
Dead Woman's Lane
PR 5
P
Walk 12
LEY GREEN
PR 3
'Red Lion'
C.W.E.
'Plough'

69

WALK 12   Preston

Length of Walk: (A) 8.4 miles / 13.6 Km
                    (B) 5.9 miles / 9.5 Km
Starting Point: ´Red Lion`, Preston.
Grid Ref: TL180247
Maps: OS Landranger Sheet 166
         OS Explorer Sheet 193
         Chiltern Society FP Map No.29
How to get there / Parking: Preston, some 2.5 miles south of
     Hitchin, may be reached from Hitchin Hill Roundabout at
     the junction of the A602 and B656 by taking the road sign-
     posted to Gosmore for 2.4 miles, passing through Gosmore
     and continuing straight on to Preston. At the village green,
     find a suitable parking space in the side roads around it, but
     do **not** use the pub car park without the landlord's
     permission.
Notes: Heavy nettle growth may be encountered in several
places on both walks in the summer months.

Preston, with its leafy green with an attractive well and pub, is the epitome of the English village. Like most villages, it has a long history, its manor of ´Deneslai` being listed in the Domesday Book. In 1147, the manor was given to the Knights Templar, an order of warrior-monks, who held it till their suppression in 1312, and thus it became known as Temple Dinsley. Subsequently the manor was held by another monastic order called the Knights Hospitaller before it fell to the Crown in the Reformation. The present house called Temple Dinsley, built in 1714 and greatly enlarged by Sir Edwin Lutyens in 1908, is now a private girls' school, but the fact that it is on the site of the ancient monastery was proved in 1902 when a thirteenth-century stone coffin lid bearing the emblem of the Knights Templar was unearthed in the gardens and this is now preserved in the parish church built in 1900. The vicinity of Preston, however, also has other religious associations as nearby Wain Wood was the scene of secret midnight services with massive congregations held by the Puritan writer and preacher John Bunyan, author of ´Pilgrim's Progress`, while Castle Farm stands on the site of Hunsdon House, whose non-conformist occupants also suffered seventeenth-century religious persecution. This same house was converted in the 1760s to resemble a castle (hence the name of the farm) by Captain Robert Hinde, an eccentric retired army officer, whom the contemporary author, Laurence Sterne took as the model for Uncle Toby in his `Tristram Shandy`.

Both walks take the Chiltern Way Extension eastwards from Preston, dropping with fine views into the Ippolyts valley at Chapelfoot before turning south by way of the ruins of Minsden Chapel and the hamlet of Langley End to reach St. Paul's Walden, childhood home and possibly birthplace of the late Queen Mother. From here, Walk A continues southwards to pass through Whitwell in the picturesque Mimram valley to reach Horn Hill before leaving the Chiltern Way Extension and returning on a parallel route, while Walk B leaves the Chiltern Way Extension at St. Paul's Walden and turns west past Stagenhoe Park to rejoin Walk A and follow it on a wooded route back to Preston.

Both walks start with your back to the `Red Lion` on Preston's picturesque village green and turn right. At a T-junction, **joining the Chiltern Way Extension**, turn right into School Lane, signposted to St. Paul's Walden and Whitwell and follow it for half a mile, passing the gates of the Princess Helena College to reach a T-junction with a road called St. Alban's Highway. Here turn left towards Gosmore and Hitchin, then, after about 70 yards, turn right through a hedge gap onto path PR2, taking this fenced path past an underground reservoir. On emerging into a field, follow a right-hand hedge straight on, turning left at a corner of the field and continuing until you reach a gap in the hedge. Here transfer to the other side of the hedge and take path LA1, still following the hedge to Poynders End Farm with its converted wooden barns and timber-framed farmhouse. Go straight on past the farm, then take a grassy track beside a left-hand hedge. Where the hedge turns left, take the grassy track straight on with wide views across the valley towards Hitchin to your left and Stevenage beyond the next rise. Eventually the track joins a right-hand hedge, which you follow to the B656 at Chapelfoot.

Turn right onto this road and follow it past the `Rusty Gun`, part of which dates from the seventeenth century. At the far end of the pub garden, before reaching a black wooden barn, turn right onto bridleway LA2, joining the Hertfordshire Way, passing the end of the pub and turning left by a large chestnut tree into a fenced path. On emerging into a field, follow the left-hand hedge straight on, gently climbing. Where the hedge ends, bear slightly left, bear slightly left heading for the near left-hand corner of Minsden Chapel Plantation which conceals the chapel ruins.

Built in the fourteenth century, Minsden Chapel was a chapel-of-ease of Hitchin parish serving the lost hamlet of 'Minlesden' referred to in the Domesday Book. By 1650 the hamlet would seem to have disappeared as the chapel was already reported to be in a decayed state and during the last recorded service here, the wedding of Enoch West and Mary Horn in 1738, the curate is believed to have narrowly missed being struck by falling masonry. In the early twentieth century, the noted local historian, Reginald Hine, who was fascinated by these allegedly haunted ruins, leased them from the Church of England and subsequently had his ashes scattered here when he died in 1949.

Now follow the outside edge of the wood straight on downhill. At its far end, bear slightly left across the field then right to follow the field side of a roadside hedge to a hedge gap leading to the B651. Turn right onto this road, then fork immediately left onto bridleway LA17, climbing gently through hillside scrubland. At a T-junction of tracks, bear left, climbing more steeply to reach the end of a macadam road by Hill End Farm at Langley End. Take this road straight on, then, at a left-hand bend, fork right onto bridleway LA16, passing through a copse to enter a field. Now, with views towards Stevenage to your left, take a track beside a right-hand hedge straight on. At the far end of the field, bear right between hedges, then, where the track bears left into another field, fork right into a narrow green lane. Now follow its winding course, eventually entering a copse where you keep right at a fork and continue to Langley Lane.

Turn left onto this narrow road, then immediately right onto path LA3, leaving the wood and heading for the right-hand end of a coniferous plantation to pass through a fence gap. Now go straight on, at first skirting the conifers, then continuing ahead to join a track straight on through a copse called Hitch Spring to reach the B651, onto which you turn left, passing the lodge gates of Stagenhoe Park surmounted by stags and wrought-ironwork. Mentioned in the Domesday Book, Stagenhoe Park's present house was built in 1737 and is now a Sue Ryder Home. In the 1880s it was occupied by Sir Arthur Sullivan, who composed 'The Mikado' here and outraged local people by his lifestyle. On rounding a left-hand bend, turn right through a hedge gap onto path PW7, bearing left and following the left-hand edge of the field. On nearing a cottage, bear slightly left onto a fenced path leading to a narrow road at St. Paul's Walden.

St. Paul's Walden, set in hillside parkland above the Mimram valley in the far north-east corner of the Chilterns, is probably best known for its disputed claim to have been the birthplace in 1900 of the late Queen Mother, daughter of the Earl and Countess of Strathmore, whose family, the Bowes-Lyons (formerly Bowes), have owned St. Paul's Waldenbury for more than 200 years. The present house, which can be seen from path PW3, was built in 1767 and considerably extended in 1887. The parish church, where the Queen Mother was christened and which she attended as a child, dates from the fourteenth century and has a chancel rebuilt by Edward Gilbert in 1727. When this church was built, however, the village had another name as it was then called Abbot's Walden because the manor belonged to St. Alban's Abbey, but during the Reformation the manor passed to St. Paul's Cathedral and so was renamed St. Paul's Walden in 1544. The royal wedding in 1923 did not, however, create the village's first royal connection as there is a memorial in the church to Henry Stapleford, who died in 1631 at the age of 76 having acted as a servant to three very different monarchs: Elizabeth I, James I and Charles I.

Walk A now turns left onto this road, then omit the rest of this paragraph. **Walk B, leaving the Chiltern Way Extension**, turns right onto this road and follows it past some cottages, then bears left to a T-junction. Here turn right onto a cul-de-sac road and follow it to the end of its macadam surface at the site of an old lodge. Now, ignoring a branching path to your left and a farm road to your right, take the road's stony continuation (path PW9) straight on past Garden Wood and an unusual Jacobean cottage to reach the macadam drive to Stagenhoe Park. Turn left onto this drive (still path PW9) with views of the house to your left. Where the drive forks, fork right off it and take a grassy path beside a left-hand fence straight on to a corner of the field. Here bear half right through a belt of scrub, then ignore a crossing track and continue through a hedge gap to reach a barbed-wire fence. Now, **rejoining Walk A**, turn right onto path PW12 and read the last paragraph.

Walk A, having passed the White House, at a left-hand bend, now forks right onto path PW3, passing through the churchyard to reach gates onto another road. Cross this road and take a fenced track (still path PW3) straight on, descending gently through old parkland for a quarter mile. By a cottage called The Garden House, take a macadam drive straight on, ignoring a branching drive to the left and continuing uphill to cross an avenue of trees where you can obtain a view of St. Paul's Waldenbury to your right. Now ignore a kissing-gate to your left and on rounding a right-hand bend, fork left through a kissing-gate by a field gate, then fork left again onto fenced path PW2, which later starts to descend with views of Whitwell in the Mimram valley opening out ahead and reaches a crossing farm road. Here keep straight on to a gate and kissing-gate leading to a footbridge over the River Mimram (until recent years often given the alternative name of Maran). Cross this bridge and bear slightly left across a field to a gate and kissing-gate, then follow a rough drive bearing right to reach the B651, Whitwell High Street.

Whitwell, locally pronounced `Whi'll`, in the picturesque Mimram valley, has long been famous for its watercress and was, at one time, also a centre of straw plaiting for the Luton hat-making industry. Though always a hamlet of St. Paul's Walden parish without its own church, Whitwell appears both to be an ancient settlement and to have long been larger than the mother village as the vicinity of its narrow High Street can boast a fascinating collection of half-timbered cottages and inns, dating back in at least the case of the `Bull` to the sixteenth century, as well as some fine Georgian houses. This suggests that practical and economic factors such as a convenient water supply and its location on an ancient valley bottom road from Hatfield towards Bedford and not just a displacement of population to create the park at St. Paul's Waldenbury may be the reason for its size.

Turn right onto the B651, then, after 90 yards, turn left onto path PW32, following a grassy sunken way, which soon becomes enclosed between hedges and fences, uphill, ignoring a branching path to your right and eventually emerging into a field. Here, leaving the Hertfordshire Way, turn right onto bridleway PW34, following the right-hand hedge and later ignoring a crossing path (**where you join Walk 13**) and reaching a corner of the field. Now keep straight on along a green lane to reach the car park off Bradway. At its far side, turn left onto enclosed macadam path PW28, soon passing a recreation ground to your left and the end of a residential cul-de-sac to your right. At the far end of the recreation ground, the path becomes enclosed by hedges and bears right then left to meet a road called Hill View, onto which you turn right to reach the B651, Horn Hill. Turn left onto this road, leaving Whitwell, soon with fine views to your right up Lilley Bottom.

Just past a water tower, at a sharp left-hand bend, **leaving the Chiltern Way Extension, Walk 13** and the B651, turn sharp right onto byway PW36, following a sunken track downhill through a strip of woodland, then continuing along a green lane, eventually with views opening out to your right towards Whitwell. On reaching Bendish Lane, cross it and take a sunken lane straight on downhill to Lilley Bottom Road. Turn left onto this, crossing a bridge over the River Mimram, then, just past the entrance to Nine Wells Watercress Farm, turn right onto path PW12, following a flint track gently uphill for half a mile with views towards Whitwell to your right. At the top of the hill, go through a hedge gap and take a grassy track beside a right-hand fence straight on, gradually bearing left, soon with a fine view of Stagenhoe Park emerging from behind a copse ahead. Near the bottom of a dip, go through gates and bear half right onto a low causeway across the valley bottom. On nearing a dead tree, go

74

WALK 12

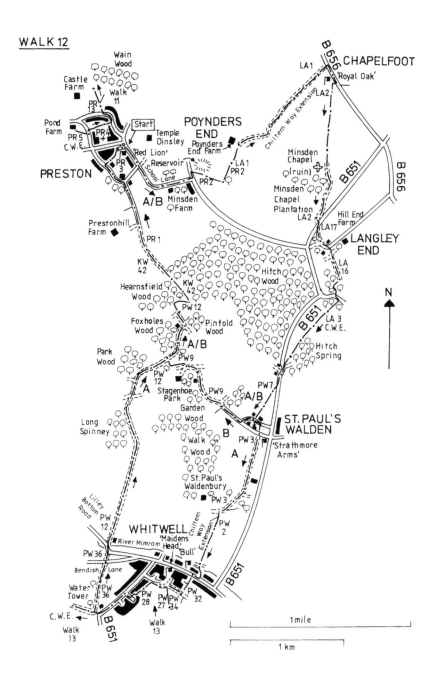

through further gates and bear slightly left into a sunken way uphill into the right-hand corner of Park Wood. Now, ignoring a branching track to your left, continue along a sunken track through the wood, then along a narrow sunken green lane to reach a waymarked junction where you keep straight on, **rejoining Walk B**.

Walks A and B now take path PW12 straight on through Foxholes Wood, eventually bearing left and emerging into a field. Here follow a grassy track straight on along the outside edge of the wood and past a cottage to reach a farm road. Turn left onto this, passing the front of a cottage and ignoring a branching path to your right, then continue downhill to pass left of a copse and go through a hedge gap. Here fork right, immediately bearing left and following a right-hand hedge uphill to the edge of Hearnsfield Wood. Do **not** enter this wood, but turn right through a hedge gap and follow the outside edge of the wood. After 150 yards, after rounding a slight left-hand bend in the wood edge, turn sharp left through a hedge gap into the wood and ignoring a branching path to your right, take path KW42, following a right-hand fence straight on through the wood. At the far side of the wood, continue along an old green lane which later bears right (becoming path PR1) and eventually emerges onto a bend in a road. Take this road straight on for a quarter mile, then, at a fork, keep left and continue for a further 250 yards. Just past the entrance to Preston Primary School, turn right onto path PR3 and follow this enclosed macadam path to the end of a lane, along which you continue to your starting point.

WALK 13   Kimpton

Length of Walk: 6.3 miles / 10.1 Km
Starting Point: ´The Boot`, Kimpton.
Grid Ref: TL174183
Maps: OS Landranger Sheet 166
OS Explorer Sheets 182 & 193
Chiltern Society FP Maps Nos. 29 & 30
How to get there / Parking: Kimpton, 5 miles southeast of
Luton, may be reached from the town by taking the B653
towards Wheathampstead for 1.7 miles. Now turn left onto
a road signposted to Kimpton/Peter's Green and follow it for
3.4 miles. On the edge of Kimpton, turn left onto the B652,
then, just past ´The Boot`, either park in a long parking bay
to your left or turn left into Park Lane and find a suitable
parking space in the residential side-streets.

Kimpton, only reached by winding narrow roads in a remote
shallow bottom where the Chiltern downslope gives way to the
rolling hills of central Hertfordshire, was once described as a
´sleepy little village`. No doubt this was formerly true as pre-war
maps show Kimpton as merely a straggle of cottages along the
village High Street and it is only since the war that it has been
swamped with modern housing. Aside from the old buildings along
High Street, some from the sixteenth to eighteenth centuries,
Kimpton can also boast a twelfth-century church with thirteenth-
century murals and a fifteenth-century tower and small spire known
as a ´Hertfordshire spike`.

The walk, which is easy in nature in dry weather but may
become more heavy-going when the ground is wet, first takes you
northwards over a low open ridge with wide views in places, to join
the Chiltern Way Extension at Whitwell in the Mimram valley. You
then follow the Way southwestwards across remote hills towards
Peter's Green, before leaving the Way, turning southeastwards and
returning via Ansells End to Kimpton.

Starting with your back to ´The Boot` in Kimpton High Street (B652),
bear left, then turn left into Park Lane. Disregard Canham Close to
your right and then turn right onto path KM34, a tarmac alleyway,
ignoring branching paths to left and right. After 200 yards, at the far

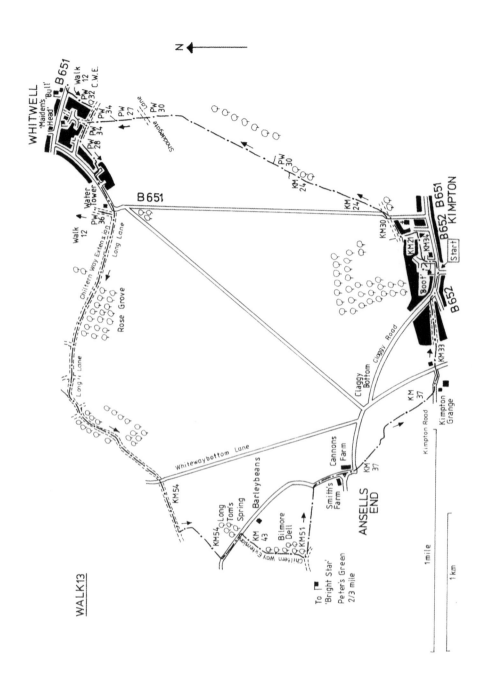

WALK 13

N ←

WHITWELL
'Maiden's
Head' 'Bull'
B 651
Walk 12
PW 32 C.W.E.
PW 34
PW 28 34 PW
PW 27
PW 30
Snookspate Lane

B 651

Water
Tower
PW 36
Walk 12
Chiltern Way Extension
Long Lane

Rose Grove

Long Lane

Whitewaybottom Lane

KM 54

KM 54
Long
Tom's
Spring
KM 43
Biltmore
Dell
KM 51
Barleybeans
Chiltern Way Extension

Cannons
Farm
Smith's
Farm
ANSELLS
END
KM 37

To
'Bright Star'
Peter's Green
2/3 mile

Claggy
Bottom
Claggy Road

KM 24
KM 24
PW 30

KM 30
KM 21
KM 31
Start
Boot
B 652
KIMPTON
B 651
B 652

KM 33

KM 37

Kimpton
Grange

Kimpton Road

1 mile

1 km

78

end of a small green to your left, do **not** join Church Lane, but turn left onto path KM21, following a slightly sunken way along the edge of the green, eventually passing under an archway in a tall hedge. Now go straight on, ignoring a crossing path and a branching path to your left. Just before a small gate, turn right onto fenced path KM30 and follow it for nearly 200 yards to the B651. Turn left onto this road, then, at a left-hand bend, take path KM25 straight on along a private road. Where the left-hand hedge gives way to an open field, bear slightly left onto path KM24 across the field with views to your right towards the Mimram valley, eventually joining and following the left side of a copse. At the far end of the copse, take path PW30 straight on to a hedge gap between oak trees, then, joining the Hertfordshire Way, bear slightly right across the next field over the brow of the hill, with St. Paul's Walden Church soon coming into view slightly to your left in trees on the skyline. Eventually you go through a gap in a sporadic hedge in the next dip, then bear half left up the next field and over a rise where the outskirts of Whitwell come into view to your left, then head for the corner of a hedge. Here cross a rough track known as Shacklegate Lane and take path PW27 straight on through a hedge gap, heading for an electricity pole left of a cluster of pale red roofs at Whitwell, then, leaving the Hertfordshire Way, continue to a second pole by a gap in the far hedge on the edge of the village.

Whitwell, locally pronounced ´Whi'll`, in the picturesque Mimram valley has long been famous for its watercress and was, at one time, also a centre of straw plaiting for the Luton hat-making industry. Though always a hamlet of St. Paul's Walden parish without its own church, Whitwell appears both to be an ancient settlement and to have long been larger than the mother village as the vicinity of its narrow High Street can boast a fascinating collection of half-timbered cottages and inns, dating back in at least the case of the ´Bull` to the sixteenth century, as well as some fine Georgian houses. This suggests that practical and economic factors such as a convenient water supply and its location on an ancient valley bottom road from Hatfield towards Bedford and not just a displacement of population to create the park at St. Paul's Waldenbury may be the reason for its size.

Now, **joining the Chiltern Way Extension and Walk 12**, turn left onto bridleway PW34, following a right-hand hedge, then a wall to reach a corner of the field. Here keep straight on along a green lane to a car park. At its far side, turn left onto enclosed macadam path PW28, soon passing a recreation ground to your left and the end of a residential cul-de-sac to your right. At the far end of the recreation ground, the path becomes enclosed by hedges and bears right then left to meet a road called Hill View, onto which you turn right to reach the B651, Horn Hill. Turn left onto this road, leaving Whitwell, soon with fine views to your right up Lilley Bottom. Just past a water tower, at a sharp left-hand bend, **leave** the B651 (and **Walk 12**) and take Long Lane, the left-hand of two green lanes, bearing slightly right. Now follow this unmade public road for one mile, enclosed by hedges at first, then passing a wood called Rose Grove to your left before becoming open and continuing, ignoring all branching or crossing tracks or paths, finally keeping left at a fork to enter a sunken lane. On reemerging into a field, take a fenced track straight on, keeping right of the hedge ahead and following it then a line of trees along the valley bottom to a gap in a transverse hedge. Now bear slightly left and take a gravel track downhill and up again to a hedge gap leading to Whitewaybottom Lane.

Cross this road and take path KM54 straight on through a gap by a gate opposite, then gently uphill beside a right-hand hedge. At the far end of the field, turn left and follow the near side of the hedge uphill. At the top of the hill, where the hedge bears left, turn right through a gap in it and go straight on across the field, with views towards Breachwood Green over your right shoulder, to reach a gap in the far hedge leading to a narrow road. Turn left onto this road, then, after nearly 300 yards, at a slight left-hand bend by the far side of a copse called Long Tom's Spring, turn right through a gap by a gate and take path KM43, following the right-hand side of a hedge with views towards Peter's Green on the ridge ahead. On reaching a scrubby copse called Bilmore Dell, bear half left and follow its outside edge downhill into a valley bottom.

Here, **leaving the Chiltern Way Extension**, turn left onto bridleway KM51, following a left-hand hedge. Where the hedge wiggles to the right, go straight on through a bridlegate in it and follow its other side for a quarter mile to a bridlegate onto a narrow road. Turn right onto this and follow it uphill to a road junction at Ansells End. Here go straight on, then, halfway round a left-hand bend, turn right through a hedge gap onto path KM37, going straight across a field with views across Kimpton to your left to reach a corner of the far hedge left of a gap by an oak tree. Now bear slightly left and follow the hedge for a quarter mile. Where the hedge ends, bear slightly left along what is normally a crop-break to an old field boundary where you cross a low boundary bank and continue across a field to reach Kimpton Road by a large cottage. Turn left onto this road, then, at a junction, take bridleway KM33 straight on through a hedge gap and follow a left-hand hedge across a field to the edge of Kimpton. Here continue between back garden fences, eventually joining a macadam path which leads you to Claggy Road. Turn right onto this road, then immediately left onto the B652 to reach your starting point.

WALK 14   Luton

Length of Walk: 7.0 miles / 11.3 Km
Starting Point: Main entrance to Luton Airport Parkway
Station.
Grid Ref: TL105205
Maps: OS Landranger Sheet 166
OS Explorer Sheets 182 & 193
Chiltern Society FP Map No.30
Parking: There is a multi-storey car park by Luton Airport
Parkway Station which is signposted off the roundabout at
the junction of the A1081 spur and B653.

Luton, a large industrial town probably now best known for its airport specialising in low-cost flights, may seem an unlikely (and indeed unpromising) starting point for a country walk, but the town situated in a gap in the Chiltern escarpment created by the Lea valley is surrounded by fine walking country including spectacular downland and a combination of the M1, Luton Hoo Park and the airport have effectively prevented the town's expansion southwards.

While this combination also greatly restricts access for walkers from the town to its surrounding countryside, this walk takes advantage of the creation of a new railway station and associated parking facilities near the gap between the airport and Luton Hoo Park to lead you rapidly from the town into the remote upland country south of the airport, passing the fascinating mediæval ruins of Someries Castle and continuing to the tiny hamlet of Chiltern Green, where you appropriately join the Chiltern Way. From here, you follow the Way southwards with fine views across the hills, descending to East Hyde in the Lea valley where you leave the Chiltern Way again and take the Lea Valley Walk along the course of a disused railway line to return to Luton.

Starting from the main entrance to Luton Airport Parkway Station, take Parkway Road straight on past the multi-storey car park to reach a roundabout. Here turn left onto a macadam path beside the B653 towards Wheathampstead. Having passed under the A1081 (Airport Way) bridge, fork left onto a macadamed cycle track up a slope. At the top of the rise, turn left up two flights of steps, then turn left again onto a tarmac path, immediately bearing right and climbing to join the A1081 footway. Follow this over a railway bridge, then, at a gap in the right-hand crash barrier, turn right onto path HY4 up a flight of steps to reach a squeeze-stile by a corner of the Luton Airport perimeter fence directly beneath the flightpath. Now follow this fence, soon bearing left and later right and descending into a valley. Here turn left and continue to follow the airport perimeter fence until a padlocked gate bars your way ahead. Pass right of this gate and follow a left-hand barbed-wire fence for over 300 yards to reach a gate and kissing-gate in a field corner near Someries Farm and the ruins of Someries Castle.

What remains today are the ruins of the gatehouse of a red-brick fortified manor house built by Lord John Wenlock between 1448 and 1459 and a red-brick chapel added between 1463 and his death at the Battle of Tewkesbury in 1471. The main house was, however, demolished by John Napier in 1742 and its bricks were reused to build Someries Farm. The site of a previous thirteenth-century fortified manor house is also nearby, but, despite the name, there is never thought to have been a castle here.

Now go through the kissing-gate, then bear half right to pass between the farmhouse and the ruins and reach a gate and kissing-gate. Here bear half right onto a farm road and follow it for a quarter mile, later with views towards Luton Hoo to your right. On reaching the end of a public macadam road, turn left onto path HY5, following the right-hand side of a sporadic line of trees. At the far side of the field, go through a hedge gap into an old green lane (bridleway HY2), then turn right and follow it for two-thirds of a mile. Where it eventually bears left and narrows, you continue through a tree belt, briefly joining the edge of a field to your right, then reentering the tree belt to reach a road. Now turn right onto this, passing through a copse to reach Chiltern Green, ignoring Copt Hall Road to your right by the half-timbered Chiltern Green Farmhouse and continuing to a T-junction. Here bear slightly right across Chiltern Green towards a cottage with a white gable end, where you bear left onto bridleway HY6, following a rough road past some cottages.

Soon after leaving the cottages behind, **joining the Chiltern Way**, turn right through a kissing-gate onto path HY9, bearing slightly left through bushes, then following a left-hand fence to two more kissing-gates. Now follow the right-hand side of a field boundary straight on for nearly a quarter mile, with views of Luton Hoo to your right and The Hyde to your left opening out at the top of a rise.

Luton Hoo, in its extensive park laid out by Capability Brown, was originally designed in 1767 by Robert Adam for the third Earl of Bute, George III's first prime minister and a keen botanist, who was instrumental in the establishment of Kew Gardens. Following two extensive fires, however, it had to be remodelled in 1903, while an earlier house on the same site is said to have been the birthplace in 1507 of Anne Boleyn, one of the six ill-fated queens of Henry VIII. The Hyde, though less pretentious in scale, is also of Georgian origin.

On reaching a line of oak trees, keep left of them, soon with a new hedge to your left, then follow this hedge for a third of a mile until you pass right of a large clump of trees. At a waymarked junction turn left onto path HY7, following a grassy track past the back of the clump. After 300 yards, turn right onto path HY8, following a grassy track downhill towards the turret of East Hyde's red-brick Italianate church in the Lea valley, built by Ferrey in 1841, eventually reaching a hedge at the edge of the village by a tall oak tree. Here turn left and follow the hedge to Farr's Lane, then turn right down the lane to reach a staggered crossroads with the B653.

The village of East Hyde, extending along the B653 in the Lea valley, barely existed in the early nineteenth century, but the coming of the railways with no fewer than two railway stations would seem to have led to its expansion. First the Great Northern Railway built a branch line from Welwyn Garden City up the Lea valley to Luton and Dunstable in 1860 with a station at East Hyde known as Luton Hoo and then, in 1868, the Midland Railway built their St. Pancras - Bedford main line, nicknamed the 'Bed-Pan Line' with a station at East Hyde known as Chiltern Green. While the old GNR branch line with Luton Hoo Station was closed by Dr. Beeching in 1962, the Midland Railway station had already been closed and so all that now remains is one main line with no station, but much of the old branch line has since become part of the Lea Valley Walk and a cycle track.

Turn right onto the B653, then left into Thrales End Lane, crossing a bridge over the River Lea. Now, **leaving the Chiltern Way**, turn right onto the cycle track and footpath following the old GNR line, soon passing under a railway bridge bearing the St. Pancras main line and continuing for three quarters of a mile, passing a sewage works, eventually descending a slope and passing through scrub before entering a cutting leading to the site of Luton Hoo Station where the platform can still be seen to your left together with an attractive fenced-off station house. At the far end of the station, go through a gap by a gate onto the West Hyde road, then turn left then immediately right onto the continuation of the cycle track, following the left-hand edge of the old railway line beside the sewage works fence to cross bridges over the River Lea and the B653, where Sustrans has had to build a new bridge to replace the old railway bridge which was demolished many years ago.

Now continue along the railway embankment through woodland, soon entering a cutting. Where the railway fence bars your way ahead, bear slightly left down a slope to pass through safety barriers and cross Copt Hall Road, where the old railway bridge can be seen to your right. Now take a fenced track straight on beside the St. Pancras railway for nearly a mile with views to your left across Luton Hoo Park and towards Luton, ignoring a crossing track, a branching path to your left and a flight of steps to your left. At a fork by a gate to your left, keep left, soon joining the B653 to pass under the A1081 bridge and reach the roundabout, where you turn right into Parkway Road for your starting point.

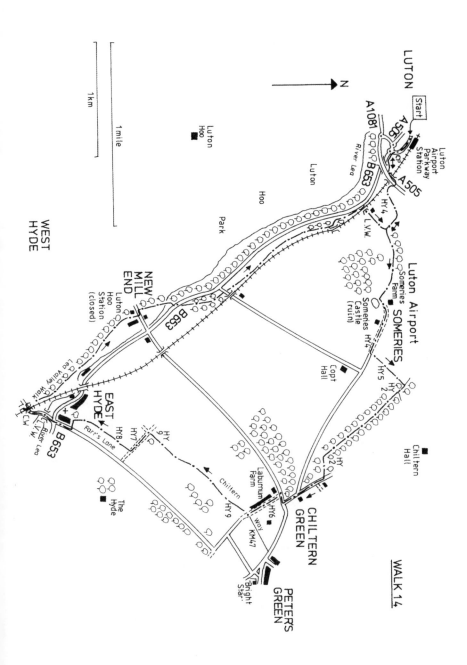

WALK 14

85

WALK 15   Flamstead

Length of Walk: 6.9 miles / 11.1 Km
Starting Point: ´Three Blackbirds`, Flamstead.
Grid Ref: TL078146
Maps: OS Landranger Sheet 166
OS Explorer Sheet 182
Chiltern Society FP Maps Nos. 20, 21 & 27
How to get there / Parking: Flamstead, 4 miles south of Luton,
may be reached by leaving the M1 at Junction 9 and taking
the A5 towards Dunstable, almost immediately turning left at
the first turning signposted to Flamstead. At a T-junction in
the village by the ´Three Blackbirds`, turn right into Chapel
Road, then take the first turning left (Friendless Lane) where
you can park.
Notes: Heavy nettle growth may be encountered in places in the
summer months, particularly on paths FS45 and FS16.

Flamstead, a corruption of ´Verlamstead`, on its hilltop above the
Ver valley, has an attractive village centre with half-timbered and
flint cottages and a row of almshouses dating from 1669, but is
dominated, when seen from afar, by its magnificent twelfth-century
church with a massive tower incorporating Roman bricks and a
small mediæval spire known as a ´Hertfordshire spike`. The church
also boasts some of the finest mediæval murals in Hertfordshire,
which were only rediscovered in about 1930, as well as exquisite
seventeenth- and eighteenth-century marble monuments by Stanton
and Flaxman and is the burial place of the founder of the renowned
transport firm, Thomas Pickford, who died in 1811. Despite being
less than a mile from both the M1 and the A5, Flamstead has
remained a remarkably quiet, rural village and, with its open, hilly
surroundings, offers a selection of pleasant walks with fine views.
    From Flamstead, the walk takes the Chiltern Way southwest-
wards across the remote plateau separating the Ver and Gade
valleys towards Gaddesden Row with wide views across the hills in
a number of places. You then leave the Way and turn north to pass
through Beechwood Park with its imposing 300-year-old mansion
before crossing a ridge with more fine views to reach Markyate on
the slopes of the Ver valley and turn southeast along this open ridge
back to Flamstead.

Starting from the road junction by the 'Three Blackbirds' at Flamstead, take Trowley Hill Road past the church to **join the Chiltern Way**, then turn right onto path FS32, a fenced alleyway leading you out past a housing estate into a field. Now go straight on across the field, passing an electricity pole and then heading for a hedge gap left of an ash tree in tall bushes ahead. Go through this gap and turn left onto a narrow road called Pietley Hill. At a left-hand bend, turn right through a hedge gap onto path FS37 downhill to pass a signpost at the bottom, then go straight on uphill to a gap in the top hedge leading to Wood End Lane where there is a fine view behind you back across the valley to Flamstead.

Go through this gap, then turn right into Wood End Lane. Just after Scratch Wood begins to your left, turn right through a gap by a gate and take path FS45, bearing slightly left across a field to the near corner of a wood called Yewtree Spring. Here keep right of the wood and follow its outside edge to a waymarked fence gap leading into it. Turn left through this and take the waymarked path through the wood, which is carpeted with bluebells in April and May, to reach a fence gap at the far corner into a field. Here bear slightly right across the field to the corner of a hedge, with views ahead across these remote hills towards the distant Bedfordshire village of Studham. Now bear left and follow the hedge to pass through a kissing-gate in it, then follow its other side. On nearing Little Woodend Cottages, go through another kissing-gate and keep left of a shed to join a drive by the cottages, then take this drive straight on to reach Puddephat's Lane.

Now, **leaving the Chiltern Way**, turn right onto this road and follow it for over a third of a mile to a staggered road junction in the bottom of a dip. Here turn left through lodge gates onto path FS56, taking the drive to Beechwood Park School through parkland landscaped by Capability Brown. On nearing the school, ignore a signposted branching path to your left and, now on path FS47, continue to follow the drive, bearing right, ignoring branching drives to your left and passing the front of the mansion, built in chequered brick with stone dressings in 1702 near the site of a twelfth-century Benedictine nunnery. Where the macadam drive turns left, leave it and take a gravel track straight on, keeping right at a further fork and continuing for nearly half a mile until you reach a crossways just beyond Kennels Lodge. Here turn right into a rough lane (still path FS47) and follow it for over half a mile, passing Beechwood Home Farm and Gravelpit Wood to your left and crossing a valley to reach a gate leading to the end of the macadamed section of Roe End Lane on the next ridge. Turn right onto this road, passing Roe End Farm to your left, then, just past Spring Cottage to your right, turn left through a kissing-gate onto path MY17 following a right-hand hedge. After a quarter mile, where the hedge bears left, bear half right through a hedge gap and take what is normally a grass crop-break straight on towards Markyate, soon joining the left-hand side of a hedge. At the far end of the field on the edge of the village, bear left and follow a right-hand hedge downhill to a fence gap, then turn right through a kissing-gate to reach the end of Parkfield Road in Markyate.

Markyate, formerly Markyate Street or even Market Street, grew up as a long straggle of mainly eighteenth-century buildings along Watling Street, now High Street, which till 1897 formed the boundary between Hertfordshire and Bedfordshire. Although the village was bypassed by the modern A5 in 1957, (which, due to its narrowness, had been the only main road in England to have a 15-m.p.h. speed limit!), a number of coaching inns still bear witness to the fact that the main road used to run through the village. The bypass, however, cut off the nearby manor house known as Markyate Cell (built in 1539 on the site of a mediæval nunnery, hence its name) and the nearby church dating from 1734 from the rest of the village. In 1605 the sixteenth-century 'Sun Inn' was the scene of the arrest of a servant of Ambrose Rookwood, one of the conspirators in the Gunpowder Plot and it is also claimed that the highwayman, Dick Turpin once stayed here. Legend further has it that Lady Katherine Ferrers, a seventeenth-century widow from Markyate Cell, became a highway-man who met a violent death and her ghost is said to haunt the house and the A5.

Take Parkfield Road straight on. At a left-hand bend, turn right up steps onto fenced path MY24 leading uphill to Pickford Road, which reminds us that it was in Markyate that the transport firm was originally based. Turn left onto this and follow it downhill for 150 yards, then, at the far end of a row of cottages to your right, turn right onto path MY20, passing right of a garage with a blue door to enter a sunken way leading uphill. At a fork, keep right, passing through a squeeze-stile and soon entering a field. Now follow a right-hand hedge gently uphill past allotments. By the far end of the allotments, bear left, still following the right-hand hedge uphill with wide views opening out to your left down the Ver valley towards Flamstead and the M1.

At the top of the hill, turn right onto a crossing track, then follow it, bearing left once again with a hedge to your right, soon on path FS17. Where the track and hedge turn right, leave them and go straight on across a large field, heading just left of the right-hand end of a tree belt to reach a gap in the trees just left of a kink. Now bear slightly right across the next field to a kissing-gate, then bear slightly

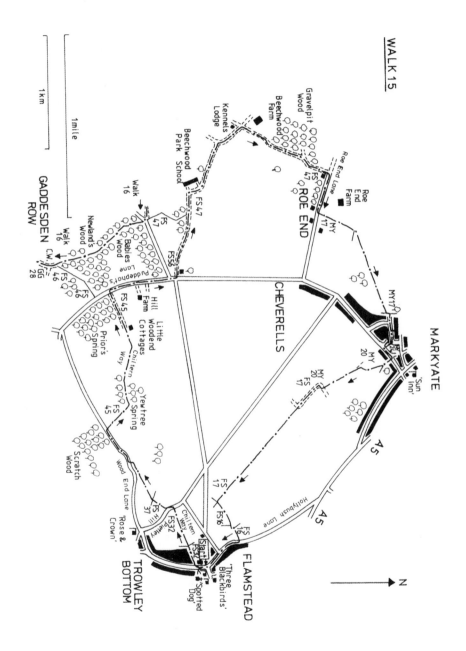

WALK 15

1km

1mile

GADDESDEN ROW

Walk 16

Newland's Wood

Walk 16

Babies Wood

C.W.
GG
28

FS 46

FS 46

Gravelpit Wood

Beechwood Farm

Kennels Lodge

Beechwood Park School

FS 47

FS 47

FS 47

FS 56

Puddephat's Lane

Hill Farm

Little Woodend Cottages

Chiltern Way

Prior's Spring

FS 45

Yewtree Spring

FS 45

Scratch Wood

Wood End Lane

FS 37 Hill

'Rose & Crown'

Chiltern Way

FS 32

FS 32

Start

Three Blackbirds'

'Spotted Dog'

FLAMSTEAD

TROWLEY BOTTOM

FS 9

FS 56

FS 17

FS 17

Hollybush Lane

A5

A5

MY 20

MY 20

MY 17

'Sun Inn'

MARKYATE

MY 17

CHEVERELLS

Roe End Farm

ROE END

MY 17

Roe End Lane

FS 47

N

89

right, following a left-hand fence across another field to another kissing-gate and a small gate in the next hedge. Here follow a left-hand hedge straight on to a small gate, then turn left onto path FS16, crossing a farm track, passing through a kissing-gate and following a left-hand hedge to a kissing-gate in a field corner leading to a fenced path. Take this path round a field corner, then turn right through a kissing-gate and bear slightly left across a field to cross a stile by overgrown gates left of cream cottages in Hollybush Lane on the edge of Flamstead. Now turn right onto this road and follow it uphill back to your starting point.

WALK 16   Gaddesden Row

Length of Walk: 6.4 miles / 10.3 Km
Starting Point: Car park outside Gaddesden Row School.
Grid Ref: TL050130
Maps: OS Landranger Sheet 166
       OS Explorer Sheet 182
       Chiltern Society FP Map No. 20
How to get there / Parking: Gaddesden Row School, 4 miles
north of Hemel Hempstead, may be reached from the town
by taking the A4146 towards Leighton Buzzard to the ´Red
Lion` at Water End. Here turn right onto the road signposted
to Flamstead and Markyate and follow it for 1.8 miles to a
T-junction at Gaddesden Row. Now turn left and follow the
road for 500 yards, looking out for a sign to Gaddesden
Row J.M.I. School where there is a small car park to your
right.
Notes: Heavy nettle growth may be encountered in places in the
summer months.

Gaddesden Row, in the parish of Great Gaddesden, is an unusual
settlement, comprising a series of isolated farms and cottages
ranged along a two-mile-long ridgetop road with the hamlet of
Jockey End at its northwest end. Despite its scattered nature,
Gaddesden Row would, however, seem to have been populated
since the Stone Age, as Stone Age flints, tools and weapons have
been found here.

Its mother village of Great Gaddesden, which you visit during
the course of the walk and which, like so many ´great` villages, is
smaller than its ´little` namesake, is set in an idyllic location in the
Gade valley, but the picturesque cluster of church, farm, school and
cottages is marred by an insensitive council house development
tacked onto it. In the past, Great Gaddesden was very much the
estate village of the Halseys, who have lived here since 1512, still
have a large estate here and continue to live at Gaddesden Place.
This Palladian mansion was built for the Halseys between 1768 and
1773 by James Wyatt, designer of Ashridge, to replace their
previous house, the Golden Parsonage, of which only a wing from
1705 remains, while the church contains the eighteenth-century
Halsey Chapel with over twenty monuments to family members

including examples of the work of Rysbrack and Flaxman. The twelfth-century church is also noted for the use of Roman bricks from a nearby villa in its construction and its massive fifteenth-century tower with some fearsome gargoyles.

The walk takes the Chiltern Way from Gaddesden Row across an upland plateau passing the Golden Parsonage and Gaddesden Place before descending into the Gade valley at the picturesque hamlet of Water End. You then leave the Way and climb through woodland to Piper's Hill, before turning north, recrossing the Gade valley at Great Gaddesden with fine views and continuing across the upland plateau to Jockey End, then circling back to rejoin the Chiltern Way and reach your starting point.

Starting from the car park by Gaddesden Row School, **follow the Chiltern Way**, crossing the road and taking path GG23 straight on along the drive to The Lane House. On reaching a gate and kissing-gate, turn left beside a right-hand hedge to a field corner. Here turn right through a hedge gap and continue to a kissing-gate into a parkland field with a view ahead of the Golden Parsonage. Now bear half right across two fields, later with fine views of the Golden Parsonage to your left, to reach gates in the far hedge at a junction of farm tracks. Here bear half right onto a track, following a right-hand hedge to reach a corner of Marsh Wood. Now fork right onto a track into the wood and follow it straight on, ignoring a branching track to your right, passing Home Farm to your left and then disregarding a crossing track, to reach a gate into a field.

Here keep straight on, passing just left of a wooden electricity pole, then following a power line with views to the right across the Gade valley. Soon on path GG18, by the third electricity pole, bear slightly left to a set of gates in a slight dip and follow a right-hand fence uphill to reach a pair of metal gates in the fence. Turn right through these onto path GG21, bearing slightly left to reach gates in the next fence. Now keep straight on, aiming left of a cream cottage with a gable at Water End in the Gade valley when this comes into view, with Gaddesden Place emerging from the trees to your left. Having passed through a small gate, keep straight on through the middle of a copse after which superb views open out across the picturesque hamlet of Water End with its seventeenth-century brick-and-timber cottages below you and towards Great Gaddesden with its prominent church to your right. Now go through another gate and continue downhill to a kissing-gate by the near left-hand corner of the cream cottage, then take a fenced path to a gate onto the A4146.

Cross this road with great care (beware of the blind bend to your left!), then turn right onto its footway. After 10 yards, turn left onto path GG66 down an alleyway to a kissing-gate into a riverside meadow. Here bear half right, following a right-hand fence at first to a footbridge over the Gade, then, **leaving the Chiltern Way**, take path GG67, bearing slightly right to reach a small gate by an electricity pole. Go through this, then fork left onto a fenced path beside a right-hand hedge leading uphill into Highpark Wood. In the wood, keep straight on uphill at first, then levelling out. After a quarter mile, where the path forks either side of a small pit, fork right then right again onto path GG71, leaving the wood and following a right-hand hedge towards the top of Piper's Hill. After 250 yards, turn right through a hedge gap onto path GG72, following a left-hand hedge with fine views ahead across the Gade valley towards Gaddesden Place. At the far end of the field, just past an oak tree, go straight on through a wide hedge gap, then turn left, following the left-hand hedge to pass through a kissing-gate. Now bear right and follow a right-hand hedge to a gate and kissing-gate into a green lane leading to a road on the edge of Great Gaddesden opposite a Victorian postbox.

Turn right onto this road, then, after 30 yards, turn left up a flight of steps onto fenced path GG2 leading to a stile. Turn right over this and follow a left-hand fence downhill to two kissing-gates into the extension of Great Gaddesden churchyard, then follow a right-hand fence straight on to the wall of the old churchyard. Here disregard a stile and turn left, following the wall to a kissing-gate. Now ignore a kissing-gate to your right and follow the right-hand fence straight on past a row of garages to reach a stile. Turn right over this to join an estate road and follow it, bearing left then right to reach a small green to your left. Here leave the road and take the continuation of path GG2, bearing slightly left across the green to a kissing-gate into a riverside meadow, then bear half left to pass the corner of a hedge and follow the hedge to a gate. Do **not** go through this gate, but turn right and follow a left-hand fence to a floodwalk and footbridges over the River Gade, then continue to a kissing-gate onto the A4146.

Cross this road and take path GG4 straight on along a concrete drive. Where the drive turns left, take a grassy track straight on beside a right-hand hedge, soon bearing left. Where this hedge turns right, keep straight on uphill across the field to a hedge gap and kissing-gate leading into Hoo Wood. Just inside the wood, fork right onto path GG16, following the inside edge of the wood to a kissing-gate, then continuing along its outside edge to a gate and a kissing-gate then further gates into a parkland field. Now follow a right-hand fence straight on through two parkland fields, then, by a junction of fences and a pair of wooden gates to your right where the Old Hoo can be seen through the trees to your right, take path GG80 straight on past the Old Hoo, soon leaving the fence behind and heading for gates in the next hedge. Here take restricted byway GG14 straight on following a right-hand hedge. Where this hedge turns right, take path GG13 straight on across the field to a gap in the next hedge, then bear slightly left across the next field to a kissing-gate by the corner of a hedge. Here bear slightly right across a further field to cross a stile between gates under an oak tree in the far hedge. Now follow a right-hand hedge straight on through allotments to a gate and stile onto the Gaddesden Row road on the edge of Jockey End.

Here turn left onto macadam path GG75 beside the road. Where this path ends, cross the road and take path GG9 through gates opposite into a recreation ground, then follow its left-hand hedge to pass through a gate at the far side. Now follow a left-hand fence straight on. Where it turns left, take what is normally an uncultivated crop-break straight on downhill into Ballingdon Bottom. Here descend steps in a hedge gap into Dean Lane (byway GG73), then turn right and follow this green lane for over a third of a mile to reach a bend in a road. Now bear right, crossing the road and taking restricted byway FS57 into and uphill through Babies Wood. At the far side of the wood, keep straight on within a tree belt, eventually entering and passing through Newland's Wood, then continuing within another tree belt until a wide track merges through gates from your left. Here, **rejoining the Chiltern Way**, take restricted byway FS57 straight on along a green lane. Where the lane forks, bear half right, taking restricted byway GG82 along its continuation to reach your starting point.

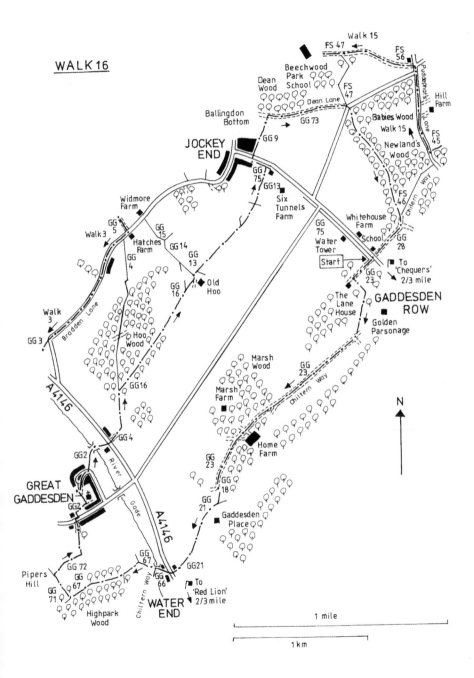

WALK 16

WALK 17   Hemel Hempstead Station

Length of Walk: 7.0 miles / 11.4 Km
Starting Point: Main entrance to Hemel Hempstead Station.
Grid Ref: TL043059
Maps: OS Landranger Sheet 166
OS Explorer Sheet 182
Chiltern Society FP Maps Nos. 5, 17 & 20
Parking: Hemel Hempstead Station is located just off the A4251 at Boxmoor about 1 mile southwest of the town centre. At the roundabout by the station, turn off the main road into Fishery Road, crossing Boxmoor Common and the canal bridge by the ´Fishery Inn`, then seek an on-street parking space in one of the side streets.

Since the war, Hemel Hempstead, at the confluence of the rivers Gade and Bulbourne, has developed into a large modern town due to its designation as a ´new town`. Despite this, the surrounding countryside has retained its rural atmosphere and even the town itself is less of a concrete jungle than some of its counterparts, thanks to the preservation of ´green lungs`, particularly along the river valleys. In fact, Hemel Hempstead, has a long history as the A4251, on which the station is situated, is part of a Roman road known as Akeman Street and remains of Roman villas have been found not only here but also in Gadebridge Park to the north of the town centre. In the Middle Ages, Hemel Hempstead must already have been a wealthy market town (as is attested by its magnificent twelfth-century church) and in the eighteenth and nineteenth centuries the construction of the Grand Junction Canal, the L&NWR main line from London (Euston) to the Midlands and North and several paper mills where modern paper-making methods were pioneered, all to the south of the mediæval town, caused its expansion southwards and the absorption of neighbouring villages such as Boxmoor where the railway station is situated.

The walk takes the Chiltern Way southwestwards, soon leaving the town behind and climbing the wooded southern slope of the Bulbourne valley to Felden and the rural upland plateau beyond. Leaving the Way, you then turn northwest crossing a valley to reach the Little Hay Golf Course near Westbrook Hay, where there are fine views across the Bulbourne valley, and continuing with

more fine views in places, eventually crossing the Bourne Gutter valley and A41 to reach Sugar Lane on a ridge near Berkhamsted. Now turning east, you follow this green lane along the ridge with fine views in places, finally descending to Bourne End in the Bulbourne valley where you join the Grand Union Canal towpath and follow this peaceful waterway past picturesque Winkwell, eventually rejoining the Chiltern Way and returning to Hemel Hempstead Station.

Starting from the main entrance to Hemel Hempstead Station, turn left down the station approach to reach a roundabout. Here cross the A4251 left of the roundabout and turn left onto its footway passing under three bridges carrying the railway and the A41. Now recross the main road and, **joining the main route of the Chiltern Way**, take fenced path HH136 off the left-hand end of Meadow Way. By a subway to your left, bear half right onto path HH99, passing between bollards and ignoring a gravel lane to your right, then take an enclosed path uphill to a kissing-gate into woodland on Roughdown Common. Here fork right onto path HH100 climbing gently through the wood and soon passing between bollards onto a cobbled then flinty drive. Soon after this drive bears right, fork left onto a woodland path, climbing gently to reach another flinty track (byway HH101), then turn right onto this to reach Felden Lane.

Now turn left into Felden Lane, then, just past Roefields Close, fork right onto path HH105 along the macadam drive to Felden Lodge through woodland onto a golf course. By a single ash tree to your right, leave the drive and bear half left across a fairway to a kissing-gate in the top hedge. Here cross a bridleway and go through a kissing-gate opposite, then bear slightly right across a meadow past the corner of a garden hedge to your right to a kissing-gate by a tall cypress tree. Now cross a cottage drive and follow a left-hand hedge straight on to a stile, then follow a right-hand hedge across a field to a squeeze-stile leading to Longcroft Lane. Turn right into it passing Felden Barns. At a left-hand bend, fork right through a kissing-gate onto path HH112 following what is normally a crop-break straight on across a field (soon on path BV16) to a gap in the next hedge. Now bear slightly right across the next field to join the edge of Bury Wood to your right level with a large clump of bushes to your left concealing a pond. Here ignore a branching path into the wood and follow its outside edge to its far end in the bottom of a dip.

Here, **leaving the Chiltern Way**, turn right onto path BV18 following a left-hand fence along the edge of the wood to a bend in a private macadam road. Take this road straight on downhill (soon on path HH111) to reach the B4505 (Box Lane) in the valley bottom.

Cross this road bearing slightly left and take a signposted permissive bridleway through a gate virtually opposite. (NB Should the permissive bridleway be closed, turn left along the B4505 for over half a mile to the entrance of Little Hay Golf Course, then turn right then immediately left onto bridleway BV30 to rejoin the normal walk route at Bourne End Lane). Now ignore a kissing-gate to your left and follow the fenced bridleway uphill beside a right-hand hedge. Near the top where the bridleway turns right, turn left through a kissing-gate then immediately right, resuming your previous direction and heading for a group of Scots pines in a tree belt ahead to reach another kissing-gate leading into a green lane. Turn right into this lane joining another permissive bridleway, then, at a track junction by a brick stable building, ignore gates to your left and bear slightly left onto a fenced track, passing left of a seat with views to your right across the Bulbourne valley towards Potten End and the western suburbs of Hemel Hempstead.

On reaching the drive to Westbrook Hay, an early nineteenth-century mansion, at one time housing the offices of the Hemel Hempstead New Town Development Corporation which supervised the construction of the new town, take a green lane straight on. At the far end of this lane where the bridleway turns right, take path BV24 straight on through a fence gap and continue through scrub, with views of Westbrook Hay and its magnificent cedar of Lebanon to your left. At the top of a slight rise by a small oak tree and a three-way signpost, bear slightly left onto path BV23 following a left-hand fence along the edge of Little Hay Golf Course. On crossing a golfers' path, take a worn grassy track straight on. Soon after the track bears left by a pair of cypresses, turn right by a signpost onto a permissive path, crossing a golfers' path then keeping left of an iron fence to enter Hanging Wood. Just inside the wood keep left at a fork, then by a deep pit to your right, keep right at another fork, bearing right and dropping through the wood. At a track junction take a permissive bridleway straight on, gradually bearing left to reach a gate and motorcycle trap leading to Bourne End Lane.

Turn left onto this cul-de-sac road, following it uphill through the wood, then gradually levelling out with fine views across the hills to your right. On passing a large house and a bungalow, at the end of the public road, turn right over a stile onto path BV29 and follow a right-hand hedge. At the far end of the field turn right through a hedge gap then left and follow the edge of a tree belt, then a wood, gently downhill to cross a concealed stile in a crossing hedge. Now bear half right and follow a left-hand hedge over a hill to a gate and stile onto a macadam farm road. Take this road (bridleway BV26) straight on, then, at a left-hand bend near Lower Farm, fork right onto

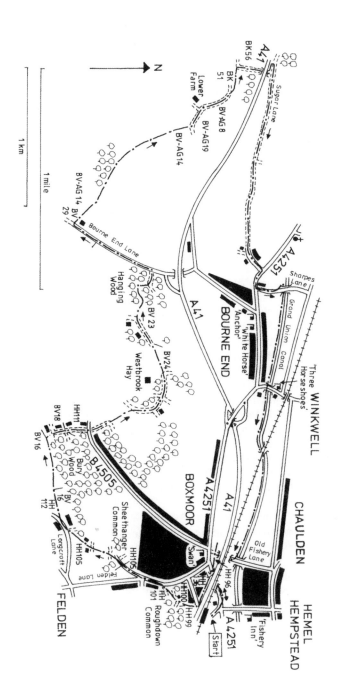

BERKHAMSTED

BOVINGDON

N

1 km

1 mile

BK56

A41

BK 51

Lower Farm

BV-AG 8

BV-AG19

BV-AG14

BV-AG 14 BV. 29

Sugar Lane

Bourne End Lane

Hanging Wood

A41

BV 23

Westbrook Hay

BV24

"Anchor"

"White Horse"

BOURNE END

Sharpes Lane

A4251

Grand Union Canal

Three Horseshoes

WINKWELL

BV18

HH111

BV 16

Bury Wood

B4505

BV 16

HH 112

Longcroft Lane

Felden Lane

Sheethanger Common

HH105

HH105

A4251

BOXMOOR

A41

A4251

"Swan"

Old Fishery Lane

HH100

HH 99

HH 101

Roughdown Common

FELDEN

CHAULDEN

HH 96

"Fishery Inn"

A4251

Start

HEMEL HEMPSTEAD

99

bridleway BV35 taking a fenced grassy track towards a field gate. Just before this gate, fork right through a bridlegate and follow a left-hand hedge. Where this hedge bears left, leave it and take bridleway BK51 straight on across the field, which is occasionally flooded by the upper reaches of the fitfully-flowing Bourne Gutter, to a barbed-wire fence, then bear left and follow it to a bridlegate. Turn right through this, then fork right onto path BK56 following a grassy track beside a right-hand hedge uphill to pass a copse, then continue ahead to a tunnel under the A41. At the far end of the tunnel bear left up a ramp, then continue between the A41 fence and a hedge to a kissing-gate leading to Sugar Lane. Turn sharp right into this green lane and follow it for nearly a mile, eventually reaching some bungalows on the edge of Bourne End where the lane becomes macadamed and bears left descending to the A4251.

Bourne End, straddling the old main road from London to the Midlands and Northwest midway between Berkhamsted and Hemel Hempstead, grew up around its ancient coaching inns and watermill, now part of a modern hotel. The main part of the village with its remaining inns is to your right, while 300 yards to your left is the somewhat isolated roadside church built in 1854 by the renowned Victorian architect, Sir George Gilbert Scott, better known for designing the Albert Memorial and the Midland Grand Hotel, which forms the façade of St. Pancras Station.

Cross the A4251 and turn right onto its footway, then, after rounding a left-hand bend, turn left into Sharpes Lane, soon crossing a bridge over the River Bulbourne and passing Cress Farm to your left. Now, on approaching a narrow bridge over the Grand Union Canal, fork left down a ramp onto its towpath, then turn right under the bridge and continue for nearly half a mile past two locks to cross a road by the picturesque 'Three Horseshoes' and swing-bridge at Winkwell. Here continue along the towpath for a further three-quarters of a mile passing under a railway bridge. On approaching the Old Fishery Lane bridge, turn right onto a rough fenced track to join the cul-de-sac road near its end and **rejoin the Chiltern Way**. At the end of the road, go straight on through gates and under the West Coast main line and A41. At the far end of the tunnel, go through gates, then turn left through a kissing-gate onto path HH96, following a left-hand fence to a kissing-gate onto the A4251, onto which you turn left. Now retrace your steps to Hemel Hempstead Station.

WALK 18   Chipperfield

Length of Walk: 5.5 miles / 8.8 Km
Starting Point: ´Two Brewers` crossroads, Chipperfield.
Grid Ref: TL044017
Maps: OS Landranger Sheet 166
OS Explorer Sheet 182
Chiltern Society FP Map No.5
How to get there / Parking: Chipperfield, 3 miles south of
Hemel Hempstead, may be reached from the town by taking
the A4251 towards Watford to King's Langley. In the village
centre, turn right into Vicarage Lane (signposted to Chipper-
field, Sarratt and Bovingdon) and continue for 2 miles to the
´Royal Oak` crossroads in Chipperfield. Here turn left, then,
at the next crossroads, turn right for a car park near the
church.
Notes: Heavy nettle growth may be encountered on path BV1
near Cottingham Farm in the summer months.

Chipperfield, with its extensive wooded common, has much in its
midst to make it the epitome of the traditional English village. In the
village centre is a picturesque cricket green flanked by a sixteenth-
century inn and the flint church, built in 1837 as a chapel-of-ease to
King's Langley, but later with its own parish, while along nearby
lanes are a sixteenth-century farmhouse and a manor house of
similar age with a red-brick façade added in 1716. On the common
are a number of ancient trees including several Spanish sweet
chestnuts of considerable girth; and the Apostles' Pond, so called
because of the ring of twelve ancient lime which once surrounded it
and had to be replaced in 1984.

The walk, which is of an easy nature, first leads you westwards
from Chipperfield across a gently undulating plateau to join the
Chiltern Way and follow it southeastwards through remote country
by way of Flaunden towards Sarratt before leaving the Way again
and turning east, then north, crossing Chipperfield's wooded
common to return to your starting point.

Starting from the crossroads by the ´Two Brewers`, take path CF5
diagonally across the village green to the left-hand corner of the
churchyard wall, then bear slightly right and follow this wall into

101

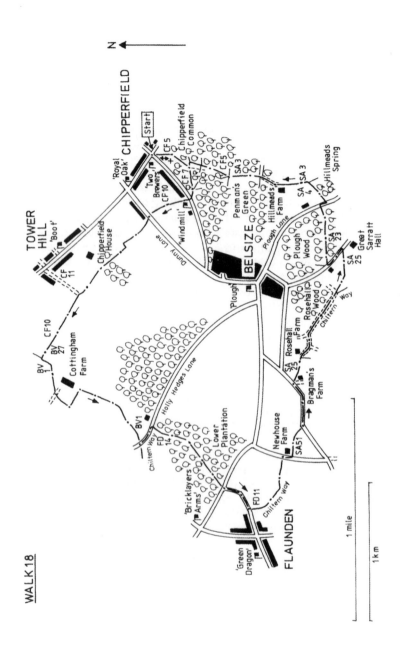

WALK 18

woodland. Having passed the church to your right, the path then leaves the wall and bears slightly left through the woods. After about 150 yards, turn right onto obvious crossing path CF7. After another 200 yards, at a T-junction of worn paths at the edge of the wood, go straight on across a small green passing left of a cedar tree to reach a road by a speed limit sign near the ´Windmill` pub which stands on or near the site of a windmill shown on the 1822 Ordnance Survey map.

Cross this road and take narrow fenced path CF10 left of The Laurels between gardens to a kissing-gate into a field where a fine view opens out ahead. Now bear slightly right down the field heading for the first pair of cottages in a row to reach a gate and kissing-gate into Dunny Lane. Bear slightly left across this road to a gate and gap leading into another field, then follow the right-hand hedge uphill through two fields, bearing left then right in the second field to enter a copse called Warefield Spring. Go straight on through this copse, then go through a kissing-gate and follow the right-hand hedge straight on. Halfway across the field, transfer through gates to the other side of the hedge and continue to a gate and kissing-gate into the end of a green lane leading to Tower Hill.

Now bear left through a hedge gap and follow what is normally a crop-break across the field to a corner of a hedge. Here follow a left-hand hedge straight on. Where the hedge ends, take path BV27 following what is normally a crop-break straight on to pass through a gap in a crossing hedge. Now turn left onto path BV1 following a left-hand hedge for 130 yards to a large gap in the hedge. Here bear half right across the field to a hedge gap some way right of a barn at Cottingham Farm. Go through this, cross a farm road and continue straight on, keeping left of a hedge. At the far side of the field go straight on through a hedge gap then turn left and follow a left-hand hedge to pass through a hedge gap in the field corner. Now turn right and follow a right-hand hedge for 400 yards then pass through a gap in this hedge and follow its other side for a further 250 yards to gates into Holly Hedges Lane.

Joining the Chiltern Way, turn left onto this narrow road. After 170 yards, where woodland commences to your right, turn right through gates onto path FD14, a fenced track along the edge of the wood, to the far side of a right-hand field, then keep straight on through the wood to a kissing-gate left of a gate leading to a road junction. Here cross the priority road and take the Flaunden road straight on gently uphill to reach the Flaunden village nameboard.

Flaunden, locally pronounced ´Flarnden`, is an unspoilt secluded village clustered around a crossroads of narrow lanes on a hilltop north of the Chess valley. The village church, built in 1838 to replace a thirteenth-century predecessor over a mile away in the Chess valley and now in Bucks, is notable for being the first to be designed by the celebrated architect, Sir George Gilbert Scott, who was later responsible for the Albert Memorial and Midland Grand Hotel which forms the façade of St. Pancras Station. This church incorporates several items from its predecessor including its fifteenth-century font, three ancient bells and the one-handed church clock.

Just past the Flaunden village nameboard where the road widens, turn left through gates onto path FD11 following a right-hand hedge gently uphill to a kissing-gate. Now bear half left across the next field heading for a gap between trees to another kissing-gate, then take a fenced path beside a left-hand hedge to reach a narrow lane. Turn right onto this road passing Newhouse Farm then turn left through a hedge gap and kissing-gate onto path SA51 following a left-hand hedge to cross a stile. Now bear slightly right across a field to a stile and steps leading down into a narrow lane. Turn left onto this road, then, after some 350 yards at the entrance to Great Bragman's Farm, fork right through a small gate onto path SA25 bearing slightly right across a field to a concealed kissing-gate at the far end of a weatherboarded barn where the timber-framed farmhouse can be seen to your right. Now follow a hedged path straight on, crossing a stile and continuing to Rosehall Farm. Here ignore a branching path to your right, then, by an entrance to the farm bear slightly right along the concrete road, bearing slightly left at one fork and slightly right at a second and continuing along a rough road, soon passing Rosehall Wood to your left and a belt of trees to your right. Now ignore a gate to your right and where the farm road turns left, leave it, crossing a stile by a gate under an oak tree.

Here, **leaving the Chiltern Way** but still on path SA25, bear slightly left across a field heading for a hedge gap through which Great Sarratt Hall can be seen ahead. Now go through a kissing-gate and bear half left across the next field to a wooden gate in the far corner, then bear half left across a further field to a kissing-gate and steps leading to a road. Turn left onto this road, then, just past Great Sarratt Hall Cottage to your left, turn right through a hedge gap into Plough Wood, immediately forking right onto path SA23 and following the inside edge of the wood to a stile into Plough Lane. Turn right onto this road, then, after 50 yards, turn left up steps and over a stile and take fenced path SA4 uphill to the near left-hand corner of a copse called Hillmeads Spring. Here cross another stile and follow the outside edge of the copse, then a sporadic line of trees to your right uphill to reach a barbed-wire fence at the top. Now turn left onto path SA3 following the fence and later a hedge to a gate and stile, then take a grassy track straight on past Hillmeads Farm to a kissing-gate just left of a black weatherboarded barn. Here turn right onto the farm drive and follow it into woodland at Penman's Green. Where this macadam drive bears right, leave it and go straight on through a squeeze-stile into a path enclosed by hedges and fences leading to a gate and squeeze-stile at the edge of woodland on Chipperfield Common. Here ignore a crossing path and permissive bridleway and take path CF5, the right-hand and wider of two waymarked paths, into woodland ignoring all crossing and branching paths and tracks. After 350 yards at a T-junction, by a seat and wooden signpost, turn left, then, after 40 yards at a crossways, turn right rejoining your outward route and following it back past the church to your starting point.

WALK 19　　　　　　　　　　　Chorleywood

Length of Walk: 6.6 miles / 10.6 Km
Starting Point:　　Entrance to the car park by Chorleywood
　　　　　　　　　　　Church.
Grid Ref:　　　　TQ036966
Maps:　OS Landranger Sheet 166 or 176
　　　　　OS Explorer Sheet 172
　　　　　Chiltern Society FP Map No.28
How to get there / Parking: Chorleywood, 2 miles northwest of
　　Rickmansworth, may be reached by leaving the M25 at
　　Junction 18 and taking the A404 towards Amersham. The
　　car park is on your left just past Chorleywood Church.
Notes: Heavy nettle growth may be encountered on path CN15
　　in the summer months, while bridleway CN3 is prone to
　　deep mud, particularly in and after wet weather.

Chorleywood, with its 200-acre partially-wooded common, was, till
the arrival of the Metropolitan Railway in 1889, a tiny Hertfordshire village surrounding its Victorian church on the A404, with a
scattering of farms and cottages around the common to the south
including the farmhouse where the Quaker, William Penn (1644 -
1718), founder of the American state of Pennsylvania, was married
in 1672. The coming of the railway, however, led to the establishment of built-up areas to the east and west of the common, which
spilled over the border into Bucks, creating the curious mixture of
countryside and suburbia known as ´Metroland`, which, amongst
others, became home to the conductor, Sir Henry Wood, founder of
the Proms.

　　The walk soon leaves suburbia behind, passing through
parkland and then dropping through woodland into the beautiful
Chess valley, before following it upstream to join the Chiltern Way
below Sarratt. You now take the Way uphill through woodland to
skirt the historic Buckinghamshire village of Chenies, where you
turn south along an ancient green lane and through more
woodland to the leafy suburb of Chorleywood West. You then leave
the Chiltern Way and circle south of the built-up area with views to
the south, before passing through The Swillett and continuing across
the wooded common to your starting point.

Starting from the entrance to the car park by Chorleywood Church, designed by the well-known Victorian architect George Street in 1870, cross the A404 and turn left along its footway. Just past the offices of Chorleywood Parish Council, turn right through gates onto path CW34, keeping right of a macadam drive at first, then joining it and following it across the park of Chorleywood House with views of the house (now District Council offices) to your left. On passing through a strip of woodland, where the macadam drive bears left, turn right onto a rough track, immediately forking left along an avenue of chestnut trees. At the far end of this avenue, ignore branching paths to left and right, then keep left at a fork and continue downhill through woodland into the Chess valley. At the bottom edge of the wood turn left onto path CW2, following a green lane for 350 yards to a fence gap. Here ignore a footbridge to your right and take a fenced path straight on along the bank of the Chess, later bearing left to join a macadam drive, where you pass left of padlocked gates to reach North Hill.

Cross this road and go through a kissing-gate opposite onto path CW1, following a left-hand hedge to a gate and kissing-gate. Now continue through a hedge gap into Bucks and take path CN17, following a left-hand hedge through two disused fields. Near the far end of the second field, **joining the Chiltern Way**, turn left through a concealed kissing-gate onto path CN15 into Turvey Lane Wood. Go straight on through this wood, ignoring the kissing-gate of a branching path to your right and continuing along a track up a valley bottom for over a third of a mile, eventually emerging through a gap by an overgrown stile into a field. Here bear half left uphill to enter the right-hand corner of Wyburn Wood. Now go straight on through this wood to a gate, then take a fenced path to reach two more gates leading to a road in Chenies.

Chenies, which belonged to the Earls and Dukes of Bedford and their predecessors by marriage, the Cheyne family, from the thirteenth century till 1954, is today a picturesque model village largely rebuilt by the Estate in the nineteenth century. Its fine Manor, once known as Chenies Palace as both Henry VIII and Elizabeth I stayed there, is in part fifteenth-century, but mainly dates from 1530, when it was extended by the 1st Earl of Bedford while the fifteenth-century church is noted for the Bedford Chapel with its superb monuments dating from 1556. Originally known as Isenhampstead, the village name evolved in the thirteenth century to Isenhampstead Cheynes and only contracted to its present form in the nineteenth century.

Now cross the village street and turn right onto its footway, passing the Old Rectory. After 100 yards, where the village inns are straight ahead, turn left through a kissing-gate onto path CN25. Now follow a right-hand hedge across the cricket field then pass through a kissing-gate and continue beside the right-hand hedge. Where the hedge bears right, leave it and go straight on across two fields to a kissing-gate, then continue between a hedge and a fence to a kissing-gate onto a road where the Manor is to your right. Turn left onto this road to reach the A404. Cross this main road carefully and take bridleway CN3 straight on, entering a sunken green lane and following it gently downhill for half a mile, passing through Halsey's Wood and reaching a tunnel under the Metropolitan Line, now jointly used by Chiltern Railways.

At the far end of the tunnel go past a gate into Whitelands Wood, reentering Hertfordshire. Now ignoring a branching path to your left, take bridleway CW38 straight on along a woodland track beside a right-hand hedge, disregarding branching paths to your left. Where the hedge bears away to the right, take the track straight on downhill and up again, ignoring all branching or crossing paths or tracks to reach a gate at the edge of the wood. Here disregard a crossing path and a path forking right into a plantation and walk round the right-hand end of a gate then take a fenced track along the outside edge of Hillas Wood with Chorleywood West coming into view ahead, later leaving the wood behind and taking the fenced track straight on, passing Newhouse Farm with its tall cedar to your right. On reaching its drive (bridleway CN3a), turn left onto it (briefly reentering Bucks) and follow it to a road junction in Chorleywood West, (the name given to the part of Chorleywood, which, till 1992, was in Bucks, originally a distant outpost of Chalfont St. Peter parish and more recently part of Chenies).

Now in Hertfordshire again, cross Blacketts Wood Drive and take Chalfont Lane straight on towards The Swillett for a quarter mile to reach a T-junction. Here turn right into Shire Lane, so called because it follows the ancient county boundary. Where the priority road bears left into Heronsgate Road, leave it, forking right into Old Shire Lane (bridleway CW33). Soon reaching an unchanged section of county boundary, follow this access road (bridleway CN52/CW33) for a third of a mile. Where its macadam surface ends, **leaving the Chiltern Way and Bucks behind and joining the reverse direction of Walk 20**, turn left onto path CW23, taking a fenced path right of a sunken lane, soon diverging from the lane. On reaching a squeeze-stile, turn right into a rough lane to reach a narrow macadam lane called Bullsland Lane (bridleway CW24). Bear right onto this, following it downhill past a wood, then up again to Bullsland Farm with its half-timbered farmhouse and black weatherboarded barn. Here turn left through a

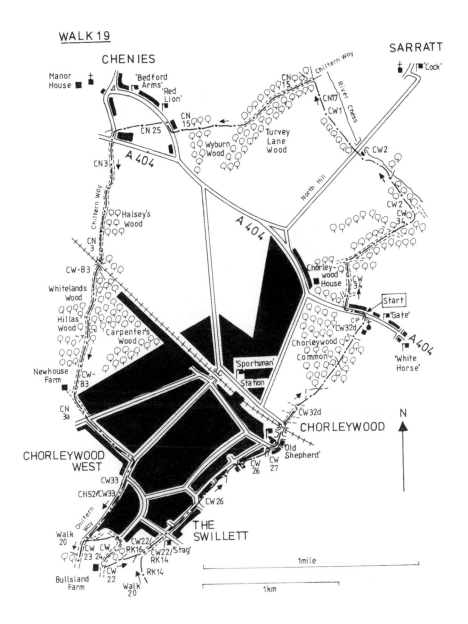

WALK 19

CHENIES

SARRATT

THE SWILLETT

CHORLEYWOOD

CHORLEYWOOD WEST

kissing-gate onto path CW22, bearing slightly left across a field to a kissing-gate by a corner of a wood. Soon diverging from the left-hand fence, take path CW22/RK16 straight on uphill to reach a kissing-gate. Now cross a fenced track and stile and continue to a second stile. Here, **leaving Walk 20**, take fenced path CW22/RK14 straight on to a road junction by ´The Stag` at The Swillett.

Now cross the priority road and take Stag Lane straight on. At a fork, bear left into Rendlesham Way, then turn immediately right onto fenced path CW26 and follow it straight on, crossing the end of a residential road. After a further 100 yards, ignore a kissing-gate to your right and bear left then right, continuing downhill to cross Windermere Close. Now keep straight on for a further 250 yards to a residential cul-de-sac (path CW27) onto which you turn left to reach a T-junction. Here turn right onto a road uphill to reach Chorleywood Common near the ´Old Shepherd`, where you ignore turnings to left and right and continue uphill to cross a railway bridge. Now leave the road and take path CW32d straight on through a car park and along a gravel track into woodland. Where the track bears right, go straight on, crossing a golf course fairway, passing left of a green and continuing along a woodland path. At a fork, keep left, then ignore all crossing or branching paths, after a third of a mile entering the back of the car park by Chorleywood Church.

WALK 20   Maple Cross

Length of Walk: 6.1 miles / 9.8 Km
Starting Point: ´Cross Inn`, Maple Cross.
Grid Ref: TQ033928
Maps: OS Landranger Sheet 176
OS Explorer Sheet 172
Chiltern Society FP Maps Nos. 22 & 28
How to get there / Parking: Maple Cross, 2 miles southwest of
Rickmansworth, may be reached from the town or Junction
17 of the M25 by taking the A412 towards Uxbridge to
Maple Cross. Here, at the traffic lights, turn right onto a
road signposted to The Chalfonts and Buckinghamshire
University College, then immediately left into a service road
where you can park.
Notes: Heavy nettle growth may be encountered in places on
paths CP9 and RK9 in the summer months.

Maple Cross, straddling the A412 North Orbital Road in the Colne
valley at the southwestern tip of Hertfordshire, today has a
suburban appearance with its pre-war ribbon development, its
modern housing estates and its industrial estate radiating from a
crossroads by the seventeenth-century ´Cross Inn`. Indeed, a study
of old maps reveals that, up to the First World War, the village,
whose name is thought to be a corruption of ´Maypole Cross`,
comprised merely the inn, several farms and a few cottages. Despite
the lack of old buildings, however, Maple Cross nevertheless has
something of architectural interest as the British headquarters of
Nissan on the edge of the village are housed in some distinctive
modern buildings which combine the functional character of
modern western offices with a pagoda-style roof reminiscent of old
Japan.

Despite the inauspicious nature of your starting point, the walk
soon leads you across the M25 into surprisingly quiet open hill
country with fine views, following a ridgetop to skirt the southern
edge of Chorleywood and join the Chiltern Way. Entering
Buckinghamshire you then pass through Newland Park, where you
can visit the Chiltern Open Air Museum and you continue to
Ashwell's Farm near Chalfont St. Giles. Leaving the Chiltern Way,
your return route then takes you across an upland plateau to the

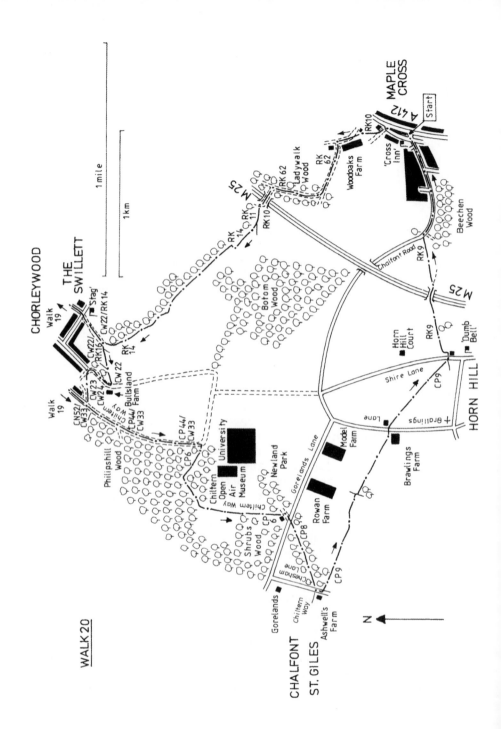

WALK 20

CHALFONT
ST. GILES

112

county boundary hamlet of Horn Hill before dropping with fine views across the Colne valley to reach Maple Cross.

Starting from the road junction near the ´Cross Inn`, take the A412 footway northwards towards Watford. Where the service road ends virtually opposite the Nissan buildings, turn left through a gate onto bridleway RK10, taking the drive to Woodoaks. After 100 yards, just past a pair of cottages to your right, leave the drive and bear slightly right across a field to gates left of a green barn at Woodoaks Farm. Now bear slightly left to pass between farm buildings, join a concrete road and follow it straight on past the farm. Just before reaching a black weatherboarded barn, turn left onto signposted bridleway RK62, passing between farm buildings and then following a grassy track beside a sporadic left-hand hedge gently uphill to enter a green lane and then a corner of Ladywalk Wood. Here, at a fork, bear right and follow a woodland track for 400 yards until you reach a bend in a stone-surfaced road. Now turn left onto this road, rejoining bridleway RK10 and crossing a bridge over the M25.

At the far end of the bridge, ignore a gate ahead and turn right, then immediately left over a stile onto path RK11, following a right-hand hedge with wide views to the south. Where the hedge bears right, continue to follow it (now on path RK14), wiggling to your right at one point. At the far end of the field, cross a stile and take a fenced path straight on for a third of a mile with views ahead towards Bullsland Farm in places. Having crossed two further stiles, look out for a stile to your right, which you cross to enter another fenced path. After 80 yards, where ´The Stag` at The Swillett is some 200 yards ahead, **joining the reverse direction of Walk 19**, turn sharp left over a stile converted from a kissing-gate onto path CW22/RK16, following a worn path to a concealed stile in the next hedge. Now go straight on through a kissing-gate and head for a white gate near a black weatherboarded gable at Bullsland Farm, passing through a kissing-gate in a dip and (now on path CW22) through another kissing-gate beside the white gate to reach a macadamed lane by the farm with its half-timbered house. Turn right into this lane (bridleway CW24) and follow it downhill and up again past a copse, then bear left to reach the end of a public road at The Swillett. Here fork left into a gravel lane, then immediately turn left through a squeeze-stile onto fenced path CW23 leading to the end of the macadamed section of Old Shire Lane, Chorleywood, which straddles the Hertfordshire/Buckinghamshire county boundary.

Leaving Walk 19 and joining the Chiltern Way, turn left into the stony continuation of this ancient lane (bridleway CN52/CW33), soon with Philipshill Wood to your right. Now keep straight on for a further half mile, ignoring all branching paths into the wood and later descending (now on bridleway CP44/CW33) into a slight valley. At the bottom of the hill, where the bridleway bears sharp left, turn right through the left-hand of two squeeze-stiles onto path CP6, entering the wood, leaving the Hertfordshire boundary behind and following a chestnut paling fence. After 300 yards you bear left and climb, now with a barbed-wire fence to your right, eventually crossing a stile into Newland Park where the Chiltern Open Air Museum can be seen to your left.

The Open Air Museum, which can be reached by turning left onto the Newland Park drive 700 yards ahead, was conceived by the Chiltern Society as a project for European Architectural Heritage Year 1975 and was founded on County Council-owned land in Newland Park the following year. Opened to the public in 1981, the constantly-expanding museum consists largely of buildings of architectural interest which would otherwise have been lost through demolition but have instead been painstakingly taken down and rebuilt at Newland Park. It is open daily from April to October from 10 a.m. to 5 p.m.

Follow the right-hand hedge then the edge of Shrubs Wood straight on through the park. At the far side of the wood bear slightly right across a field to cross a stile by a chestnut tree left of a lodge. Now turn right onto the Newland Park drive and follow it to its T-junction with Gorelands Lane. Bear slightly right across this road and take bridleway CP8 through a gap by an overgrown gate opposite, then continue for a third of a mile through a strip of woodland to reach a gap by a gate into Chesham Lane.

Leaving the Chiltern Way, turn left onto this road, passing Ashwell's Farm with its fine seventeenth-century timber-framed brick farmhouse and weatherboarded barn to your right. After 40 yards, turn left onto path CP9 into a corner of the wood, following its inside edge straight on, ignoring branching paths to right and left and eventually entering a field. Here bear right and follow a right-hand hedge towards the sprawling Rowan Farm. At the far end of the field, go through a kissing-gate and take the fenced path straight on beside a right-hand hedge past two paddocks and the farm to reach a crossing path. Here go straight on through a wooden kissing-gate and follow a left-hand hedge uphill to the top of a rise. By gates to your left, leave the hedge and go straight on across the field to a kissing-gate in the far corner, then follow a right-hand fence, later a hedge, straight on past Brawlings Farm to reach a kissing-gate into Brallings Lane. Turn right onto this road, then immediately left through a kissing-gate into a large arable field, where you bear half right, heading for a gap between pink and white cottages at Horn Hill left of the far corner of the field, when these come into view, to reach a kissing-gate opposite the pink cottage into Old Shire Lane marking the Hertfordshire boundary, where the ´Dumb Bell´ is 120 yards to your right.

At the beginning of the twentieth century, Henry Harben, who bought Newland Park together with much of the scattered hamlet of Horn Hill, in 1903, not only extended his own house but also made plans to transform Horn Hill into a model village and indeed built a fine village hall and twelve new estate cottages. Following his death in 1910 and the outbreak of the First World War, however, his son was forced to abandon the scheme before its completion.

Reentering Hertfordshire, bear half left across Shire Lane to enter narrow fenced path RK9 just left of the drive to Cross Keys Farm. Follow this path, bearing left and then right and eventually emerging through a kissing-gate into a field. Now turn right and follow a right-hand fence through two fields to a stile leading to a bridge over the M25. At the far end of the bridge, where superb views open out up and across the Colne valley towards Rickmansworth, Watford and Maple Cross, bear half left, aiming for the green roof of the Nissan building at first, then a clump of bushes on the far side of Chalfont Road in the valley bottom, to reach this road. Now turn right and follow it for half a mile into and through Maple Cross to reach your starting point.

INDEX OF PLACE NAMES

CHILTERN SOCIETY FOOTPATH MAPS

1. High Wycombe and Marlow
2. Henley and Nettlebed
3. Wendover and Princes Risborough
4. Henley and Caversham
5. Bovingdon and Abbots Langley
6. Amersham and Penn Country
7. West Wycombe and Princes Risborough
8. Chartridge and Cholesbury
9. The Oxfordshire Escarpment
10. Wallingford and Watlington
11. The Hambleden Valley
12. Hughenden Valley and Great Missenden
13. Beaconsfield and District
14. Stokenchurch and Chinnor
15. Crowmarsh and Nuffield
16. Goring and Mapledurham
17. Chesham and Berkhampstead
18. Tring and Wendover
19. Ivinghoe and Ashridge
20. Hemel Hempstead and the Gade Valley
21. The Dunstable Downs and Caddington
22. Gerrards Cross and Chalfont St. Peter
23. Toddington and Houghton Regis
24. Burnham Beeches and Stoke Poges
25. Sundon and the Barton Hills
26. Hitchin and Hexton
27. Flamstead and Redbourne
28. Rickmansworth and Chenies
29. Preston and Codicote
30. Lilley and Breachwood Green

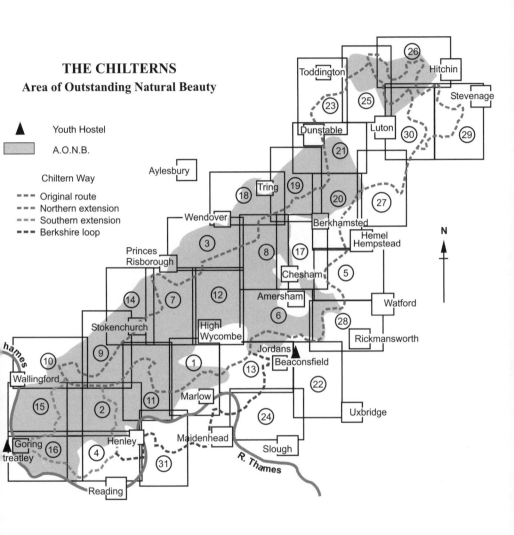

THE CHILTERNS
Area of Outstanding Natural Beauty

▲ Youth Hostel

A.O.N.B.

Chiltern Way

- - - Original route
- - - Northern extension
- - - Southern extension
- - - Berkshire loop

Toddington
Hitchin
Stevenage

26

23 25

Dunstable Luton
21 30 29

Aylesbury

18 Tring 19 20 27

Wendover Berkhamsted
Hemel
Hempstead

3 8 17

Princes
Risborough Chesham 5

14 7 12 Amersham
6 Watford

Stokenchurch 28
High
Wycombe Rickmansworth

9 Jordans
10 1 Beaconsfield
Wallingford 13 22

15 2 11 Marlow
Uxbridge

24

Goring 16 4 Henley Maidenhead
treatley Slough
31

R. Thames

Reading

N

Thames

Chiltern Society Sites

1. Bottom Wood, ancient woodland
2. Brush Hill Nature Reserve
3. Captain's Wood, woodland & nature reserve
4. Cholesbury Camp, site of iron age hill fort
5. Cobblers' Pits, woodland near Wendover Arm canal
6. Ewelme Watercress Beds & nature reserve
7. Hampden Monument, memorial to John Hampden who opposed the King's imposition of Ship Tax
8. Lacey Green Windmill, c.1650 oldest smock mill in England
9. Marlow Common (North) woodland common
10. Prestwood Nature Reserve
11. Whiteleaf Hill, historic site, chalk cross & nature reserve

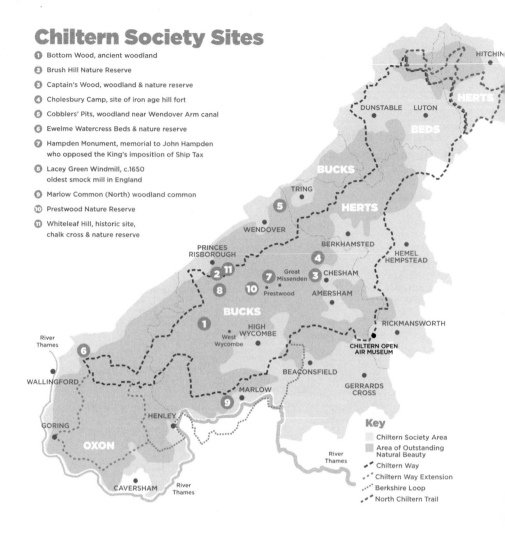

HITCHIN

HERTS

DUNSTABLE LUTON

BEDS

BUCKS

TRING

HERTS

5

WENDOVER

BERKHAMSTED

HEMEL
HEMPSTEAD

PRINCES
RISBOROUGH

4

2 11

7 Great
Missenden 3 CHESHAM

8 10 Prestwood AMERSHAM

BUCKS

1

HIGH
West WYCOMBE
Wycombe

RICKMANSWORTH

CHILTERN OPEN
AIR MUSEUM

River
Thames

6

WALLINGFORD

BEACONSFIELD

MARLOW

GERRARDS
CROSS

9

HENLEY

GORING

OXON

River
Thames

CAVERSHAM River
Thames

Key

Chiltern Society Area
Area of Outstanding
Natural Beauty
Chiltern Way
Chiltern Way Extension
Berkshire Loop
North Chiltern Trail